MEDIEVAL INTERSECTIONS

Medieval Intersections

Gender and Status in Europe in the Middle Ages

Edited by
Katherine Weikert
and Elena Woodacre

berghahn
NEW YORK • OXFORD
www.berghahnbooks.com

Published in 2021 by
Berghahn Books
www.berghahnbooks.com

© 2021 Berghahn Books

Originally published as a special issue of *Historical Reflections/Réflexions Historiques*, Volume 42, issue 1 (2016).

All rights reserved. Except for the quotation of short passages for the purposes of criticism and review, no part of this book may be reproduced in any form or by any means, electronic or mechanical, including photocopying, recording, or any information storage and retrieval system now known or to be invented, without written permission of the publisher.

Library of Congress Cataloging-in-Publication Data

Names: Weikert, Katherine, editor. | Woodacre, Elena, editor.
Title: Medieval intersections : gender and status in Europe in the Middle Ages / edited by Katherine Weikert and Elena Woodacre.
Description: New York : Berghahn Books, 2021. | "Originally published as a special issue of Historical Reflections/Réflexions Historiques, Volume 42, issue 1 (2016)"—Verso. | Includes bibliographical references and index.
Identifiers: LCCN 2021023869 | ISBN 9781800731547 (hardback) | ISBN 9781800731554 (paperback)
Subjects: LCSH: Social status—Europe—History—To 1500. | Sex role—Europe—History—To 1500. | Women—History—Middle Ages, 500–1500. | Europe—Social conditions—To 1492. | Europe—History—476–1492.
Classification: LCC HN380.Z9 S6155 2021 | DDC 305.42094—dc23
LC record available at https://lccn.loc.gov/2021023869

British Library Cataloguing in Publication Data

A catalogue record for this book is available from the British Library

ISBN 978-1-80073-154-7 hardback
ISBN 978-1-80073-155-4 paperback
ISBN 978-1-80073-156-1 ebook

Contents

List of Illustrations, Tables and Figures — vii

Preface — ix

Introduction — 1
   Gender and Status in the Medieval World
   • *Katherine Weikert and Elena Woodacre*

Chapter 1 — 8
   Mirror for Margraves: Peter Damian's Models for Male and Female Rulers
   • *Alison Creber*

Chapter 2 — 21
   Inaudito exemplo: The Abduction of Romsey's Abbess
   • *Linda D. Brown*

Chapter 3 — 35
   The Corpus Christi Devotion: Gender, Liturgy, and Authority among Dominican Nuns in Castile in the Middle Ages
   • *Mercedes Pérez Vidal*

Chapter 4 — 48
   From Villainous Letch and Sinful Outcast, to "Especially Beloved of God": Complicating the Medieval Leper through Gender and Social Status
   • *Christina Welch and Rohan Brown*

Chapter 5 — 61
   "To take a wyf": Marriage, Status, and Moral Conduct in "The Merchant's Tale"
   • *Natalie Hanna*

Chapter 6   75
Objectification, Empowerment, and the Male Gaze in the Lanval Corpus
- *Elizabeth S. Leet*

Chapter 7   88
Pueri Sunt Pueri: Machismo, Chivalry, and the Aggressive Pastimes of the Medieval Male Youth
- *Sean McGlynn*

Chapter 8   101
"And much more I am soryat for my good knyghts": Fainting, Homosociality, and Elite Male Culture in Middle English Romance
- *Rachel E. Moss*

Chapter 9   114
Wrist Clasps and Patriliny: A Hypothesis
- *Frank Battaglia*

Index   129

Illustrations, Tables and Figures

Illustrations

2.1	Grant to the Lillechurch Priory. St. John's College, Cambridge D46.27.	29
2.2	Grant to the Lillechurch Priory. St. John's College, Cambridge D46.58.	30
3.1	Corpus Christi procession in the base of the "Virgen del Pajarito," in the nuns' choir of Santo Domingo el Real de Toledo (fifteenth century).	36
3.2	San Juan Bautista de Quejana, Chapel of the Virgen del Cabello: copy made by Cristóbal González de Quesada in 1959 of the Retable and Frontal of the Life of Christ and the Virgin, now at the Chicago Art Institute.	41
3.3	Santo Domingo el Real de Toledo at the end of the sixteenth century.	42

Tables

5.1	The most frequent use of "wyf" in *The Canterbury Tales* corpus.	62
5.2	The total use of selected gender-based noun terms in "The Merchant's Tale."	63
9.1	Horse cremations at Spong Hill accompanying humans whose biological sex could be determined.	118
9.2	Spong Hill ceramics with bone-ash temper.	119

Figures

9.1 Two stages in the development of a Gloucestershure Roman Villa: with Phase II depicting an approximately first century CE structure and Phase III B probably build in the late third century. 116

9.2 Specific kinds of sleeve fasteners characterized an "Anglian" female costume [drawn by Christine Wetherell]. 121

Preface

This new edition of our collection of studies on medieval gender and status has given us the opportunity to reflect on how the field of medieval studies is continuing to address this topic in the five years since our special collection was originally published.

One aspect of medieval studies which has become increasingly important in recent years as we aim to "decolonize the curriculum" and shift traditionally Eurocentric perspectives is a move to look at the middle ages in a truly global sense. Even though the original journal edition was titled "Gender and Status in the Medieval World," our studies only represent western Europe. This is something we recognised in 2016, where we further pointed out the need for intersectionality in the fields of medieval studies, which all too often replicates itself in both scholars and scholarship. The revised title for this new edition, *Medieval Intersections: Gender and Status in Europe in the Middle Ages* reflects our geographical focus more accurately while placing emphasis on the need to "negotiate" gender and status—that these elements are flexible and fluid, and are defined by the interactions of individuals in society.

It is inspiring to see the range of excellent new scholarship arising from just the previous five years that take a diverse or global perspective on the middle ages, highlighting issues of gender and status which complement the studies in this collection. Recent volumes such as Bryan C. Keene's *Toward a Global Middle Ages* calls attention to research in medieval manuscripts from not just Europe but Asia, the Americas, Africa and Austronesia, demonstrating multidisciplinary methods to view a global medieval past through the framework of manuscript studies.[1] Established scholars such as William Chester Jordan and François Soyer have highlighted the religious diversity of medieval Europe, and problematised theories of racism and anti-Semitism in the middle ages.[2] A multitude of works specialising the medieval African continent have also been seen in the past few years, which will only improve our ability to research an inclusive past.[3] Engaging in issues of diversity in the past is not without intense scholarly debate,[4] but this should ultimately help us to enrich the development of medieval studies to recognise and celebrate its diversity in the past, present–and future.[5]

One area where an increasing diversity of studies has been particularly evident is in studies of women of the highest status—queens and elite women. A new drive to globalize queenship and royal studies can be evidenced in a recent collection on global queenship and in new works focused on royal women in the Islamic world and the Khatuns of Mongol Iran.[6] Yet even the status and perception of elite women has been challenged in recent scholarship. Since our original collection was published, Heather Tanner edited an important volume on European medieval elite women which challenges the "Exceptionalist Debate" through a series of studies demonstrating that the exercise of power by elite women was a norm rather than an anomaly.[7] Particularly relevant to this book is Theresa Earenfight's contribution, "A Lifetime of Power: Beyond Binaries of Gender," in which she examines not only the way power was exercised but how it has been described by others, which often genders and downplays the authority of women by casting it as "agency" instead.[8]

As well as continuing work nuancing the negotiations of women in the middle ages, important new works discussing European martial masculinity and research which aim to go beyond heteronormativity have been released in the last few years.[9] Ruth Mazo Karras' influential *Sexuality in Medieval Europe: Doing Unto Others* has had a 3rd edition published, providing ground-breaking studies in the history of sexuality to new scholars in the field.[10] Patricia Skinner's *Studying Gender in Medieval Europe: Historical Approaches* contains lengthy considerations of identities, categories and status, pitched at a level to engage students with these complicated concepts in order to encourage future scholarship in these areas.[11] Archaeology and literary studies, with different sources, remain largely ahead of history in pushing new directions in queering the middle ages, significantly altering paradigms.[12] For example, scholarly querying of the tenth-century viking grave at Birka, a biological female buried with warrior accoutrements, raised the possibility of new ways of seeing and interpreting non-binary identities as well as presenting new questions about the multivalent relationships between gender and status in the medieval past.[13]

Another fruitful intersection in recent scholarship has been seeking to interpret gender and status in multi- and interdisciplinary ways. Collections such as Tracy Chapman Hamilton and Mariah Proctor-Tiffany's *Moving Women, Moving Objects (400–1500)*, and Karen M. Gerhart's *Women, Rites and Ritual Objects in Premodern Japan* demonstrate that the commissioning, collection and ritual use of objects were a powerful way for women to highlight and reaffirm their status; this could be particularly powerful when connected to the elaborate rituals which marked key moments in gendered lifecycles.[14] Marguerite Keane and Mariah Proctor-Tiffany have also shown in their studies of the wills, inventories and bequests of French medieval queens how women were able to use objects to reinforce their status even after death.[15] Proctor-Tiffany notes how vital display and objects were to the performance of status for elites of both genders: "By repeating predecessors' royal behaviour, such as wearing, displaying and giving sumptuous objects, men and women could anchor themselves into royal group identity and argue for their own elevated status."[16] Recent research in spatial studies of medieval manors has been developing similar strands of argument in the Anglo-Norman sphere.[17] Indeed the spatial view of gender and place is a growing area of medieval studies, seeking the embodied experiences of space and place, exemplifying the value of interdisciplinary approaches in medieval studies.[18]

In short, the pieces referenced in this discussion demonstrate that research in medieval studies exploring issues related to both gender and status has not slowed in the five years since the initial publication of the *Historical Reflections/Réflexions Historique* issue in which these papers first appeared. The papers in this collection are part of this growing body of scholarship and reflect many of the themes highlighted in this discussion of emerging work, exploring issues of masculinity, the gendered exercise of authority, material culture and intersections between gender, space and religion, and much more. Our field continues to grow and seek new boundaries to break, with no end in sight: as research in gender and the middle ages flourishes, it becomes more diverse, more contentious, more dynamic and more exciting than ever.

Katherine Weikert is Senior Lecturer in Early Medieval European History at the University of Winchester.

Elena Woodacre is Senior Lecturer in Early Modern European History at the University of Winchester.

Notes

1. Bryan C. Keene ed., *Toward a Global Middle Ages* (Los Angeles: J. Paul Getty Museum, 2019).
2. William Chester Jordan, *The Apple of His Eye: Converts from Islam in the Reign of Louis IX*, Jews, Christians and Muslims from the Ancient to the Modern World (Princeton: Princeton University Press, 2019); François Soyer, *Medieval Antisemitism?* (Amsterdam: Amsterdam University Press, 2019).
3. See recent works such as Samantha Kelly, ed., *A Companion to Medieval Ethiopia and Eritrea* (Leiden: Brill, 2020), especially Margaux Herman's chapter 'Toward a History of Women in Medieval Ethiopia'; Michael A. Gomez, *African Dominion: A New History of Empire in Early and Medieval West Africa* (Princeton: Prince-

ton University Press, 2018); Verona Krebs, *Medieval Ethiopian Kingship, Craft and Diplomacy with Latin Europe* (London: Palgrave Macmillan, 2021); in the popular press, François-Xavier Fauvelle, *The Golden Rhinoceros: Histories of African Middle Ages*, trans. Troy Tice (Princeton: Princeton University Press, 2021).
4. See, for example, Geraldine Heng, *The Invention of Race in the Middle Ages* (Cambridge: Cambridge University Press, 2019) and S. J. Pearce, "The Inquisitor and the Moseret: *The Invention of Race in the Middle Ages* and the New English Colonialism in Jewish Historiography," *Medieval Encounters* 26:2 (2020), 145–190.
5. One such debate in the field is over the use of the term 'Anglo-Saxon.' This term has been widely recognised within North American spheres as one that often works synonymously and in tandem with racism and white supremacy. Whilst recognition of this issue is growing within Britain, the challenge to find a term to replace it is ongoing in order to not further racism and white supremacy in any part of the Anglosphere. In the light of this ongoing and significant historiographic shift, Frank Battaglia's chapter in this volume has been published here as it was originally in the 2016 journal edition in order to provide an opportunity for readers to reflect on, and to highlight, this current and important debate.
6. Elena Woodacre, ed., *A Companion to Global Queenship* (Bradford: ARC Humanities Press, 2018); Shahla Haeri, *The Unforgettable Queens of Islam: Succession, Authority, Gender* (Cambridge: CUP, 2020); De Nicola, Bruno, *Women in Mongol Iran: The Khatuns, 1206–1335* (Edinburgh: Edinburgh University Press, 2017).
7. Heather Tanner, ed., *Medieval Elite Women and the Exercise of Power, 1100–1400: Beyond the Exceptionalist Debate* (New York: Palgrave Macmillan, 2019).
8. Theresa Earenfight, "A Lifetime of Power: Beyond Binaries of Gender," in Tanner ed., *Medieval Elite Women*, 271–293.
9. Natasha R. Hodgson, Katherine J. Lewis and Matthew M. Mesley, *Crusading and Masculinities* (London: Routledge, 2019); Ann Marie Rasmussen, ed., *Rivalrous Masculinities: New Directions in Medieval Gender Studies* (South Bend, IN: Notre Dame University Press, 2019).
10. Ruth Mazo Karras, *Sexuality in Medieval Europe: Doing Onto Others*, 3rd edition (London: Routledge, 2017).
11. Patricia Skinner, *Studying Gender in Medieval Europe: Historical Approaches* (London: Palgrave, 2018).
12. For example, Will Rogers and Christopher Michael Roman, *Medieval Futurity: Essays for the Future of a Queer Medieval Studies* (DeGruyter, 2021); the establishment of the journal *Kyngervi* in 2019.
13. Neil Price et al., "Viking Warrior Women? Reassessing the Birka Chamber Grave, Bj.581," *Antiquity* 93:367 (2019), 181–198.
14. Tracy Chapman Hamilton and Mariah Proctor-Tiffany, eds., *Moving Women and Objects (400–1500)* (Leiden: Brill, 2019); *Women, Rites and Ritual Objects in Premodern Japan*, ed. Karen M. Gerhart (Leiden: Brill, 2018).
15. Marguerite Keane, *Material Culture and Queenship in 14th-Century France: The Testament of Blanche of Navarre (1331–1398)* (Leiden: Brill, 2016).
16. Mariah Proctor-Tiffany, *Medieval Art in Motion: The Inventory and Gift-Giving of Queen Clémence of Hungary* (University Park: Pennsylvania State University Press, 2019), 54.
17. Katherine Weikert, *Authority, Gender and Space in the Anglo-Norman World, 900–1200* (Woodbridge: Boydell, 2020).

18. Among others, Karen Dempsey, "Tending the 'Contested' Castle Garden: Sowing Seeds of Feminist Thought," *Cambridge Archaeological Journal*, published online 9 February 2021, 1–15; Susannah Crowder, *Performing Women: Gender, Self and Representation in Late Medieval Metz* (Manchester: Manchester University Press, 2018); Victoria Blud, Diane Heath and Einat Klafter, eds, *Gender in Medieval Places, Spaces and Thresholds* (London: Institute of Historical Research, 2018) (another publication arising from the Gender and Medieval Studies Conferences, this from 2017 at Canterbury Christ Church University).

Introduction

Gender and Status in the Medieval World

Katherine Weikert and Elena Woodacre

In January 2014, the University of Winchester hosted the Gender and Medieval Studies conference. Held sporadically since the late 1980s and, for the most part, annually in the last fifteen years, the conference series is dedicated to the study of gender in the Middle Ages. In 2014 at Winchester, the topic for discussion was "gender and status." This topic was specifically chosen for the potential fruitfulness of the idea: gender and status could encompass ideas such as social status, employment, figures of authority, marital status, legal issues, and could potentially suit any academic discipline or geographic context. The 2014 conference welcomed more than ninety scholars from throughout Europe and North America speaking on topics ranging from medieval gynecology[1] to clerical masculinity.[2] As the conference organizers noted, the large number of scholars attending and speaking on gender and status in the medieval world might indicate larger trends in medieval scholarship: that studying gender in the medieval world was no longer a niche subject, but part of the wider landscape of not just medieval studies but scholarship in general.[3]

The study of gender has indeed come a long way since its earliest inceptions in the academy and Joan Scott's appeal for scholars to consider gender as "a useful category of historical analysis."[4] Growing initially from second-wave feminism's critique of the academy and the call to recognize women's place not only in academia but in history overall, gender studies in turn grew from third-wave feminism's recognition of the value of difference with "an inclusive and non-judgmental approach that refuses to police the boundaries of the feminist political."[5] Indeed, it is only in a few far-flung corners where gender studies in history are still considered as an "add-women-and-stir" approach. Instead there is a much greater understanding that gender as a social construct—and a normative construct at that[6]—can affect all corners of life. As another structure around which we build society, this social identity impacts societal expectations of gender roles,[7] and so addressing gender as a part of a broader history should be a part of any narrative of the past. This more nuanced understanding of gender in the present, as well as in the past, has opened up many lines of enquiry that would not have been considered decades ago.

One area where this is most strongly evident is in the growing interest in masculinities as a part of gender studies of the past; the failure in some cases to include the masculine in gender studies is one of the reasons that "gender" is often presumed to be a substitute for "women."[8] Although not the sole purpose of broader studies of gender in the past, studies of masculinities in gender history helps to avoid the female-centric aims endemic in second-wave scholarship[9] and resulting claims of gynocentrism. Although not without controversy as a study of the patriarchy that initially wrought the social and power structures of gender, it is more largely recognized that the study of hegemonic masculinities can lead students and researchers to challenge this hierarchical structure, as well as recognize "complementary masculinities" that "reject gender stereotypes."[10] Furthermore, even though some regard this inclusion of studies of masculinities as a reversion to the male as the normative and controlling gender, thereby reinforcing male prerogatives, "valuable feminist scholarship on the Middle Ages ... has tended to ignore the gendered status of men; ironically privileging 'men' as universal, ahistorical, atemporal, and genderless."[11] Thus it comes as no surprise that the study of gender in the medieval world has broadened to areas previously unstudied but now considered to be a normal part of gender constructions in the past. Both the Gender and Medieval Studies conference and the collection of articles that came out of it reflect this desire to include all genders and consider the process of forming and understanding the construction of gendered identities in the Middle Ages.

Another highlight of the conference—and indeed this volume—is the importance of interdisciplinary work in medieval studies, particularly when it comes to the study of medieval gender. Many researchers seem to have taken to heart Martin Carver's plea with respect to disciplinary boundaries: "To study one discipline to the exclusion of others, on the grounds that archaeology or history or literature or art has its own theoretical framework makes no sense ... our subjects ... are what gives us our tasks ... Disciplines are simply tools, not powers."[12] When researching a subject that can be difficult to trace through singular or traditional sources, interdisciplinary research can often be the best way forward to result in fruitful academically sophisticated results. As Guy Halsall has pointed out, a more fruitful method of research would include framing the research question first, and then drawing the evidence to the question, as opposed to allowing the evidence to set the question.[13] While this has long been seen as a valid method of research in earlier medieval periods, and particularly eras when there is a perceived lack of evidence, interdisciplinary work in the whole medieval period demonstrates a rich understanding of the value of varied sources.[14]

Indeed this interdisciplinarity was evidenced throughout the conference and in this volume and scholars have embraced it in their studies of both the early and the later medieval periods. Although the tradition of interdisciplinarity was well represented, many other papers and their subsequent article versions have approached research through maintaining flexible disciplinary boundaries. These include ways of viewing theological and monastic societies, art history and history as companion disciplines, and archaeology, landscape, and history working together for larger societal questions. Medieval studies as a whole is seeking new areas to explore; while single-discipline research is still strong throughout these areas of study, scholars of gender in the medieval world have embraced interdisciplinarity as another way of demonstrating the diversity of gender in the medieval world.

Gender studies nevertheless still pushes boundaries and, by theming both the conference and this issue of *Historical Reflections/Réflexions Historique* on "Gender and Status in the Medieval World," a further aim was identified beyond the study of feminisms and masculinities: a greater depth of study of intersectionality in the medieval world. The term intersectionality was first coined by Kimberlé Crenshaw in 1991 as a way of expressing the combined oppressions of being a woman and a person of color.[15] Since then it has taken on a greater meaning in feminism and society, to broadly encompass the idea that differing forms of oppression can intersect and work together within society. Although its use and critiques of tokenism are not without value,[16] its concept in terms of seeing beyond a white, heteronormative, Christianized medieval west should be of incredible value to academics working in medieval studies.

Even though it has been utilized by numerous scholars, the term "intersectional" itself has seldom been explicitly adopted by medievalists,[17] despite work that tacitly addresses these key issues. The traditional academic approach to the past is one that narrowed the view of the medieval world, arising from an androcentric viewpoint as well as expectations about not only what the past constituted, but also the scholars who researched it.[18] This is the approach from which we strive to remove ourselves, and critiquing these viewpoints is one part of this process. Moving toward intersectionality in our work is another. Although research in the Middle Ages grows out of a system that perpetuated white, middle- and upper-class men as the primary researchers producing historical narratives about powerful men, the medieval world, as we well know, is far more than that. Discussions of intersectionality in the Middle Ages can further nuance an understanding of the past and deprivilege approaches to the medieval world that ignore or reject such nuances.

Although not explicitly addressed in the call for papers in either the conference or this special issue, the topic of "Gender and Status" gave a broad opportunity to explore overlapping identities that can result in a hierarchized and highly confining social structure. Papers and posters explored concepts such as physical impairment and life-ending illnesses in the Middle Ages;[19] queering the Middle Ages and its gender and sexual identities;[20] class structures and status;[21] and non-Christian identities in the medieval West.[22] Medieval research in gender is moving into areas of inquiry that view varying constructions of identity and how these constructions can become agents of oppression in the past, even when such intentions are not always explicit. In other words, we are seeking intersectionality, if not yet using the term. This line of research will, in the long run, only enhance our views of the past; removing a concept of a white, masculine, heteronormative Middle Ages brings the past into a clearer picture of what it meant to be a person in the Middle Ages—regardless of who that person was. Modern-day popular culture in general perpetuates this "traditional" idea of the Middle Ages;[23] by embracing and discussing intersectionality and moving areas of focus in the field, medieval studies can become more fruitful not just in scholarship but also in influencing popular perceptions of the past, a process that can make the past a far richer and more complex world to modern society.

This issue offers a diverse collection of articles that highlight the number of ways in which the term "status" can be interpreted. Instead of choosing to order the articles in the issue chronologically, we decided to organize them thematically, around different ways in which authors chose to investigate the notion of status and its relation to gender. Status can be linked to concepts of power and authority or the ideal of the "elite" in society and, indeed, there was a strong strand of papers at the conference that reflected this perception of status.[24] Two articles in this issue look specifically at high or elite status members of medieval society. Alison Creber's "Mirrors for Margraves" examines the letters of a prominent churchman, Peter Damian, to two important Italian margraves, Godfrey of Tuscany and Adelaide of Turin. Creber argues that, while Damian wrote to both with deference to their elevated status on the duties of their exalted position, Damian's advice to both margraves was deliberately framed in terms of their respective gender. Linda Brown's article also examines a woman who was high ranking in terms of both temporal and spiritual hierarchies in society, as both a princess of England and the abbess of the prominent foundation at Romsey. Brown examines the dramatic change in status of the Princess-Abbess Marie of Blois after the death of her parents and siblings made her heiress to the county of Boulogne, prompting her alleged *raptus* and disputed marriage. Marie's case emphasizes the flexibility of her status as according to secular and sacred needs, and how her social status allowed for fluid movement at times between the two offices of wife and nun-abbess.

An elevated or distinctive societal status need not be explicitly connected to the exercise of authority. Mercedes Pérez Vidal's and Christina Welch and

Rohan Brown's articles both focus on two different societal groups that seem to be held in semi-seclusion, holding little or no authority: female monastics and male lepers. While these groups appear quite divergent, these case studies reveal that they shared similarities in terms of being set apart from society, through physical separation or enclosure, and with regard to their high spiritual status, as "holy" men and women.

However, status need not be exclusively imagined in terms of social or spiritual hierarchies. Two articles, by Natalie Hanna and Elizabeth Leet, focus on marital or relationship status and how it can be reinforced by language. Both scholars undertake deep textual analysis to demonstrate how they reveal the status of relationships between men and women. In her article, Hanna examines how the terminology used by Chaucer in *Canterbury Tales* reflects the construction of marital status in late medieval England, and methods by which language could reflect systems of control. By contrast, Leet examines how both real and fairy women in Middle English Breton lays submit themselves to objectification—using interest in their bodies in order to help their lovers. By deconstructing linguistic elements of the display of the body, Leet shows how the male gaze could be used or subverted to a female end.

The final three articles all examine the construction of gender and status with an emphasis on the establishment or reinforcement of masculine ideals or patriarchal structures. Sean McGlynn examines how participation in warlike games and chivalric tournaments helped young men construct their gendered identity and status as warriors or knights. In contrast to this emphasis on aggression and perceived "manly" behavior, Rachel Moss discusses the significance of male fainting in Middle English romances. While this could be assumed to undermine or contravene expected male behavior, Moss argues that it reinforced the status of a knight, homosocial bonds, and even late medieval patriarchy itself. Frank Battaglia's article moves from textual analysis to material culture, examining the burial patterns of wrist clasps and what this reveals about concepts of gender identity, status, and an emerging system of patriliny on display through the decoration of female bodies in early Anglo-Saxon culture.

Taken together, these articles highlight the varied nuances of the concept of status and what examinations of both gender and status can reveal about medieval society. These concepts can be seen as binary: elite or low status, married or single, holy or cursed, male or female, or as complementary and cohesive as multiple parts of a societal whole. These articles also reinforce Scott's argument of the importance of gender as a category of historical analysis and the utility of a gender-based exploration of the concept of status in order to increase our knowledge and understanding of the society and culture of the Middle Ages. This special issue reflects the rich collection of scholarship that was featured at the 2014 Gender and Medieval Studies conference—and, indeed, in the tradition established by the conference series as a whole—to continually explore, discuss, and push the boundaries of gender-based studies of the medieval era.[25]

Notes

1. Lydia Harris, "Physicians, Healers and Midwives: Women in the Medieval Occupation, 1050–1350" (paper presented at the Gender and Medieval Studies Conference, University of Winchester, January 9–11, 2014).
2. Matthew Mesley, "Why German Bishops Could Not be Saved: Clerical Masculinities in the Works of Caesarius of Heisterbach" (paper presented at the Gender and Medieval Studies Conference, University of Winchester, January 9–11, 2014).
3. Katherine Weikert, "Closing Remarks," (paper presented at the Gender and Medieval Studies Conference, University of Winchester, January 9–11, 2014).
4. See Joan Wallach Scott, "Gender: A Useful Category of Historical Analysis," *American Historical Review* 91, no. 5 (1986): 1053–1076.
5. R. Clare Snyder, "What Is Third-Wave Feminism? A New Directions Essay," *Signs* 34, no. 1 (2008), accessed August 24, 2014, doi 10.1086/588436.
6. Alison Wylie, "Gender Theory and the Archaeological Record: Why Is There No Archaeology of Gender?" in *Engendering Archaeology: Women and Prehistory*, ed. J. Gero and M. Conkley (Oxford: Blackwell, 1991), 46.
7. Susan M. Johns, *Noblewomen, Aristocracy and Power in the Twelfth Century Anglo-Norman Realm*, Gender in History (Manchester: Manchester University Press, 2003), 1–7.
8. J. Wajcman, "Women and Men Managers: Careers and Equal Opportunities," in *Changing Forms of Employment, Organizations, Skills Gender*, ed. R. Cromtpon, D. Gallie, and K. Purcell (London: Routledge, 1996).
9. Amy Wharton, *The Sociology of Gender: An Introduction to Theory and Research* (Oxford: Blackwell, 2005), 5.
10. Julie Oyegun, "Working Masculinities Back into Gender," *Agenda: Empowering Women for Gender Equality* 37 (1998): 13, 18.
11. Dawn Hadley, "Introduction: Medieval Masculinities," in *Masculinities in Medieval Europe*, ed. Dawn Hadley (London: Longman, 1999), 3.
12. Martin Carver, "The Marriage of True Minds: Archaeology with Texts," in *Archaeology: The Widening Debate*, ed. Barry Cunliffe, Wendy Davies, and Colin Renfrew (London: British Academy, 2002), 498.
13. Guy Halsall, "Archaeology and Historiography," in *Companion to Historiography*, Routledge Companion Encyclopedias, ed. M. Bentley (London: Routledge, 1997), 805.
14. For examples coming solely from the discipline of history, see Guy Halsall, *Barbarian Migrations and the Roman West, 376–568* (Cambridge: Cambridge University Press, 2007); Robin Fleming, *Britain After Rome: The Fall and Rise, 400 to 1070*, Penguin History of Britain, vol. II (London: Allan Lane, 2010). An indication of rising acceptance of interdisciplinary work from historians can be seen in Fleming's 2013 MacArthur Fellows "Genius" Grant for "challenging the way historians view early medieval Britain and providing a framework for incorporating material culture into the writing of history"; "Robin Fleming," MacArthur Fellow Programme, 2 September 2013, accessed 25 August 2015, https://www.macfound.org/fellows/891/.
15. Kimberlé Crenshaw, "Mapping the Margins: Intersectionality, Identity Politics, and Violence Against Women of Color," *Stanford Law Review* 43 (1991): 1241–1299.
16. See, for example, s. e. smith, "Push(back) at the Intersections: Defining (and Critiquing) 'Intersectionality,'" *Bitch Magazine*, 5 August 2010, accessed 24 August

2015, https://bitchmedia.org/post/pushback-at-the-intersections-defining-and-critiquing-intersectionality.

17. For a limited number of examples, see M. Lindsay Kaplan, "Jessica's Mother: Medieval Constructions of Jewish Race and Gender in 'The Merchant of Venice,'" *Shakespeare Quarterly* 58, no. 1 (2007): 2, footnote 6, in criticism of the work of Lisa Lampert; Elizabeth A. Hubble, "Lettering the Self in Medieval and Early Modern France by Katherine Kong," *Medieval Feminist Forum* 47, no. 1 (2011): 86–88, accessed 24 August 2015, http://ir.uiowa.edu/mff/vol47/iss1/8, 87, noting that Kong does not address intersectionality though the topic "seems to beg for a nod" to it, 87.

18. For example, see Carl Bridenbaugh, "The Great Mutation," *American Historical Review* 68, no. 2 (1963): 315–319, implicitly outlines many of these expectations including the gender, class, and wealth of the historian.

19. Rose Drew, "Gender, Status and Impairment" (paper presented at the Gender and Medieval Studies Conference, University of Winchester, January 9–11, 2014); see also Welch and Rohan Brown, this issue.

20. Andrea-Bianka Znorovsky, "Cross-Dressing for Christ's Sake: Visualising the Sponsa in Medieval Illuminated Manuscripts" (poster presented at the Gender and Medieval Studies Conference, University of Winchester, January 9–11, 2014); Beatrice Fannon, "Masculinities in Question: Is Roland a Virgin Knight?" (paper presented at the Gender and Medieval Studies Conference, University of Winchester, January 9–11, 2014); see also Moss, this issue.

21. Sophia Germanidou, "Illustrating Women at Peasant Labour: Comparative Evidences from Medieval and Byzantine Art" (paper presented at the Gender and Medieval Studies Conference, University of Winchester, January 9–11, 2014).

22. Antonella Sciancalepore, "The Other Side of the Kingship: Saracen Ladies and Male Status in Medieval French Epics" (paper presented at the Gender and Medieval Studies Conference, University of Winchester, January 9–11, 2014).

23. For examples of three separate approaches of considering modern perceptions of the "normative" medieval, see Lillian Cespedes Gonzales, "Some Observations on Danes in Wessex Today," in *Danes in Wessex*, ed. Ryan Lavelle and Simon Roffey (Oxford: Oxbow, 2015); Katherine Weikert, "The Empress Matilda in Popular Fiction, 1970s to the Present," in *Virtuous or Villainess? The Image of the Royal Mother from the Early Medieval to the Early Modern Eras*, ed. Carey Fleiner and Elena Woodacre (Basingstoke: Palgrave Macmillan, forthcoming 2016); and Helen Young, "Place and Time: Medievalism and Making Race," *The Year's Work in Medievalism* 28 (2013): 2–6.

24. For example, see Linda E. Mitchell, "Does Social Status Trump Gender, or Vice Versa? Theoretical Approaches and the Medieval World" (paper presented at the Gender and Medieval Studies Conference, University of Winchester, January 9–11, 2014).

25. For more information on the conference series, past and present, please visit www.medievalgender.co.uk. Other publications that have been spawned from Gender and Medieval Studies conferences include Elizabeth Cox, Liz Herbert McAvoy, and Roberta Magnini, eds., *Reconsidering Gender, Time and Memory in Medieval Culture* (Woodbridge: D. S. Brewer, 2015); Diane Watt, ed., *Medieval Women in Their Communities* (Cardiff: University of Wales Press, 1997); Emma Campbell and Robert Mills, eds., *Troubled Vision: Gender, Sexuality and Sight in Medieval Text and Image* (New York: Palgrave Macmillan, 2004).

Chapter 1

Mirrors for Margraves
Peter Damian's Models for Male and Female Rulers

Alison Creber

In the early 1060s Peter Damian wrote letters on the subject of government and justice to the rulers of two Italian marks (a territorial division similar to a duchy, but situated in a borderland): Godfrey, margrave of Tuscany, and Adelaide, de facto ruler of the mark of Turin.[1] Discussions of these letters have previously focused on Damian's interaction with the laity, and of the contributions laymen and women could make to the reform church.[2] The gendered aspects of Damian's letters to Godfrey have not been studied before, but Damian's letter to Adelaide has been discussed in terms of Damian's approach to women and gender.[3] Some of these studies have downplayed the importance of gender, and characterized Damian as someone who wrote to women in the same way that he wrote to men.[4] Yet comparing and contrasting Damian's letters to Godfrey and Adelaide indicates that, although there are certain similarities, there are also striking differences between them. In this article I discuss the differing models for rule Damian offered to Godfrey and Adelaide, and his reasons for doing so. To what extent did he differentiate between them because of differences in their status or behavior, and to what extent simply because of their gender?

Peter Damian (ca. 1007–1072) was a hugely influential religious figure in the eleventh century.[5] From ca. 1035/6 he was a hermit in the eremitical community of Fonte Avellana, where he later became prior (r. 1043–1057). Damian was also active in the world as a papal legate and cardinal-bishop of Ostia (r. 1057–1067). He was also a prolific writer: there are 180 extant letters written by Damian to various individuals and institutions. In ca. 1063 and 1064 Damian wrote letters to Godfrey "the Bearded" of Lotharingia (ca. 997–1069)[6] and Adelaide of Turin (ca. 1014/24–1091),[7] both of whom ruled marks in Italy. Godfrey was originally from Upper Lotharingia: he was duke until he rebelled against Henry III of Germany (r. 1039–1056).[8] Godfrey later became margrave of Tuscany (r. 1056–1069) by marrying Beatrice (ca. 1013/26–1076), the widow of the previous margrave, Boniface of Canossa (r. ca. 1027–1052). Adelaide had inherited and was de facto ruler of the mark of Turin; through marriage she also came to rule in the county of Savoy.[9] Although her three husbands, her son, and, finally, her grandson-in-law were the titular margraves of Turin, Adelaide managed to hold and maintain power for more than fifty years.

Mirrors for Margraves

Damian frequently included exemplars in his letters to provide his correspondents with spiritual direction or to urge them to a particular course of action. His letters to Godfrey and Adelaide can be classified as a subset of the genre known as "mirrors for princes."[10] Mirrors vary quite widely, both in their content and in their sources. Essentially they are intended to provide their recipients with exemplars that reflect how they should behave according to their status in society. Mirrors for rulers are political and moral treatises that offer advice on the principles of good governance. In one of his letters to Godfrey Damian explicitly referred to his model as a "mirror." He described the virtues of Margrave Hugh of Tuscany and urged Godfrey to "hold up this predecessor of yours as a mirror."[11]

Damian's image of the ideal margrave was presented within a Christian, and specifically monastic, framework. He emphasized that both Godfrey and Adelaide should protect the poor and the weak, and be generous to the church.[12] His letters were also concerned with secular matters, and particularly with the administration of justice. Damian wrote to both Godfrey and Adelaide on the same topic of rule and justice in their respective marks, and addressed them both in the same way as "most excellent duke."[13] Nevertheless, the advice he gave them differed greatly.

In two letters to Godfrey (written ca. 1063) Damian expressed his concern that Godfrey was not doing enough to ensure that the law was properly enforced throughout his domains.[14] Damian thought that a misguided sense of piety was preventing Godfrey from ruling as he ought. He painted a bleak picture of the chaos that would ensue if Godfrey continued to allow "false" and "excessive" compassion to hinder him from administering justice.[15] First, his lands would fall into turmoil: without justice there would be violence and destruction and men would commit evil acts without fear of reprisal.[16] Second, if these "evil men" were not punished for their crimes by earthly rulers, then they would be condemned to hell hereafter.[17] This meant that, third, for bestowing false compassion on others, Godfrey himself would "incur the force of God's anger."[18] The conclusion was clear: Godfrey was to rule with severity. Yet when Damian wrote to Adelaide just a year later, he admonished her not to deal severely with those who broke the law, but to treat them with mercy and restraint.[19] He encouraged her to follow the biblical King David who did not punish Joab and Shimei in anger, but in justice (1 Kings 2:5–9). He urged Adelaide to "imitate the example of this holy king. Never abandon the practice of generosity and justice, so that following the apostolic precept 'mercy may triumph over judgment' [James 2:13]."[20]

Did Damian give this differing advice because Godfrey was ruling differently from Adelaide? There is little evidence that Godfrey was failing to administer justice in his domains. Indeed, diplomatic sources indicate that Godfrey presided over more court hearings than Adelaide.[21] Was Godfrey a more pious ruler than Adelaide? Several reform-minded writers referred to Godfrey's personal piety.[22] Yet, with the exception of Damian's letters, these accounts were written after Godfrey's death, and specifically described Godfrey's pious activities once he knew he was dying. Other narrative sources present a striking contrast between Godfrey's supposed compassion and his actual behavior. For example, Jocundus, a Lotharingian chronicler probably writing in the 1070s, explained that Godfrey was such a severe judge, even to the poor and the monasteries, that St. Servatius was forced to intervene.[23]

Damian himself may earlier have accused Godfrey of being unjust and cruel. In 1059 Damian wrote to admonish Pope Nicholas II (r. 1059–1061), who had spurned "priestly mercy" and indulged in "hostile cruelty" by imposing an interdict on the city of Ancona in order "to please one person."[24] This "one person" is not named in Damian's letter, but is generally assumed to be Godfrey, who was the prefect of the city.[25] Ancona had rebelled against Godfrey, and from Damian's letter it can be inferred that Godfrey had turned to Nicholas II for help in reasserting his position. If so, then Damian's view of Godfrey as a ruler is contradictory: in letters to Godfrey, Damian describes him as a pious ruler and urges him to govern with greater severity; elsewhere, Damian accuses Godfrey, along with Nicholas II, of being worse than tyrants, because instead of causing "the death of two or three persons," they had caused all the people of Ancona to be "excluded from the kingdom of God."[26]

Like Godfrey, Adelaide was a strong ruler who was also capable of acting ruthlessly. In 1069, for example, she sacked and burned the city of Lodi, causing the deaths of thousands of men, women, and children.[27] Few contemporaries referred to Adelaide's piety,[28] but Damian himself spoke warmly of Adelaide's protection of, and generosity to, religious institutions. He stated that of all the bishops and abbots in Adelaide's domains, the only one who criticized her in any way was the bishop of Aosta, who complained "not that he had incurred any loss on your account, but rather that his diocese had not benefitted from your generosity."[29]

Other factors must thus have affected Damian's perception of their rule. The first is location. Damian conceived of political power primarily in terms of the defense of local monasteries. He was not personally affected by developments in Turin in the northwest of Italy, and could thus urge Adelaide to be merciful. By contrast, Godfrey ruled territories where Damian's hermitage, Fonte Avellana, and its dependencies were located: disorder and lack of justice in central Italy had a direct effect on Damian and his dependents.[30] The emphasis on Godfrey's poor lordship thus indicates Damian's disappointment that Godfrey, a notable supporter of the reform church, was not a better protector of monastic lands.

Second, Damian clearly distinguished between Godfrey and Adelaide because of their gender. He suggested that a female margrave did not rule in the same way as a male margrave. Damian was a skilled rhetorician who tailored his work to suit its intended recipient.[31] His letters were not easily transferrable between his male and female correspondents even when, as in Godfrey and Adelaide's case, Damian wrote to them on the same subject. Damian clearly thought that certain virtues and exemplars were specific to women, while others were more appropriate for men. This is apparent not only from Damian's letters to Godfrey and Adelaide, but also from juxtaposing them with Damian's letters to Godfrey's wife, Beatrice of Tuscany, and to Bishop Cunibert of Turin.

Models for Godfrey

In order that he might become a better ruler, Damian urged Godfrey to follow both the models of historical rulers and precepts from the Bible. To encourage Godfrey to rule with greater severity, Damian provided him with examples of divine approval for violent acts, and made use of militaristic imagery.[32] Damian cited several biblical examples in which evildoers were "cut down by the sword" wielded by decisive judges or rulers. Thus the Amalekite who killed Saul was "cut down by David's sword," and the Apostle Peter punished Ananias and Sapphira (who did not share all their property with the church) and "cut them down with the sword to cause terror in the hearts of others who might perhaps be tempted to do the same."[33] This emphasis on the sword is Damian's. It is not found in the biblical texts he cites, which refer instead to smiting or falling down.[34] Damian used the sword as a key marker of distinction between secular and religious men: "The prince's sword is quite different from priestly symbols of dignity. You do not buckle on your sword to stroke or caress the evil deeds of violent men, but to prepare to cut them down with your weapon's flashing blows."[35] Damian clearly thought that Godfrey's "excessive" compassion was blurring the lines between secular and priestly status. He urged Godfrey to let "evil men see in you a prince, and not deride you as a priest."[36]

In his second letter to Godfrey, Damian provided further biblical examples based on paternal imagery, encouraging him to punish law-breakers. Elsewhere in his work, Damian sometimes depicted fathers as loving and affectionate,[37] but in this letter to Godfrey paternal identity is primarily associated with discipline and violence. Thus: "A father who spares the rod hates his son" (Prov. 13:24); "A man who loves his son well will whip him often" (Sir. 30:1).[38] Damian extends this analogy from fathers and sons to the relationship between a ruler and his people. Both were to oversee the moral formation of those under their care. Damian asks Godfrey: "If a father should use correction and the rod on an only son, how much more should this be true of a prince with his people, so that a great number of them should not perish in their attempt to act with unbridled liberty?"[39] Damian did not see this discipline as cruel, but as the correct response of a ruler when faced with criminal acts. Even though Damian explicitly told Godfrey not to usurp the role of the priest, he nevertheless thought that there was an eschatological dimension to Godfrey's activities as judge. If criminals were not punished for their crimes by earthly rulers, then they would "pay for [them] with eternal suffering."[40] For Damian, cruelty consisted of actions that harmed the soul, not the body, which is why he described the interdict that Nicholas II imposed on Ancona, at Godfrey's request, as cruel.

In addition to these biblical exemplars, Damian encouraged Godfrey to follow the models of the emperors Theodosius (r. 379–395)[41] and Otto III (r. 1083–1001),[42] and Hugh, margrave of Tuscany (r. ca. 969–1001).[43] Damian utilized these historical rulers to reiterate his point that Godfrey should not be overly merciful, but should use physical force to maintain discipline in his territories. He writes with approval, for example, of Otto III's blinding of his opponents and of Theodosius putting "fear into the hearts of evildoers by using the power of his imperial authority."[44] Damian's choice of exemplars was apt in several ways. First, Godfrey was clearly interested in secular models of lordship: in another letter, Damian related a story Godfrey had told him about the rule of Charlemagne (r. 768–814).[45] Second, in the story Damian recounts about Emperor Theodosius, Damian explains that Theodosius was "accustomed to talk with a certain religious hermit, whose directions the emperor used to obey."[46] This underscores the point that Godfrey should take advice from Damian, himself a hermit.[47] Third, his choice of Margrave Hugh was particularly relevant: like Hugh, Godfrey also ruled the mark of Tuscany (r. 1056–1069), the duchy of Spoleto and the mark of Camerino (r. ca. 1057/8–1069).

Hugh was not only an important model because he administered the territories that Godfrey now held, but because he had done so in an exemplary manner.[48] Hugh was generous to monasteries, had a strong commitment to justice and to good government, and dealt harshly with criminals.[49] Moreover, when Hugh felt that he could no longer administer all his domains with the necessary authority, he—supposedly willingly—renounced control of Spoleto and Camerino, and thereafter ruled only the mark of Tuscany.[50] This story reiterates Damian's criticism that Godfrey was not paying enough attention to all the territories he ruled. "I am greatly displeased," wrote Damian, "that you neglect this principality in which almost 100,000 people live."[51] Damian urged Godfrey that if he could not rule all his territories properly himself, he should "appoint a governor who will rule and administer it" for him.[52]

Godfrey was largely absent from Italy in the 1060s.[53] His wife, Beatrice, administered their Italian territories in his place. Although Godfrey gained his Italian titles and offices only through marriage to Beatrice, and although Beatrice was a more than capable ruler in her own right,[54] Damian clearly did not regard Beatrice as an acceptable substitute for Godfrey. He wrote about political issues exclusively to Godfrey, not to Beatrice. Instead Damian encouraged Beatrice to temper her husband's harshness with mercy and generosity. The image of the persuasive wife was a common trope among medieval writers, but positive "womanly influence" was strictly limited to whatever was beneficial to the church.[55] Damian offered Beatrice models of women who gave their husbands "holy advice" regarding care for the sick and the poor, and generosity to monasteries, and encouraged Beatrice to do likewise with Godfrey.[56] He also exhorted Anne, wife of Henry I of France (r. 1031–1060), and Guilla, wife of Margrave Rainer II *di Colle*, to urge their husbands to good deeds.[57] Significantly, Damian encouraged Adelaide to cultivate the same virtues of mercy and generosity as other laywomen.

Models for Adelaide

When Damian wrote to Adelaide in 1064 he did so not only to suggest how she should administer justice in her lands, but also to ask her to help enforce clerical celibacy in the mark of Turin. Damian had already written to Bishop Cunibert of Turin (r. ca. 1046–1080) on this subject,[58] but Cunibert had failed to act. So Damian wrote to Adelaide, hoping that she would galvanize Cunibert into action. This expectation was similar to Damian's belief that wives should influence their husbands for the good of the church, with one key difference. Damian envisaged most laywomen as having a narrow scope for exerting their moral influence: that is, in a domestic setting, over their husbands. By contrast, he envisaged Adelaide as legitimately exercising her influence far more widely than this. Most women were to persuade their husbands, who ruled, but Adelaide was herself a ruler.[59] In fact, in many ways, Adelaide was closer to Damian's ideal margrave than Godfrey. She was generous to monasteries. She could be relied upon in matters of clerical celibacy. And, unlike Godfrey, she managed to rule more than one territory, the mark of Turin and the county of Savoy, without the need to appoint governors to rule on her behalf.

Damian nevertheless offered Adelaide and Godfrey different models. Writing to Godfrey, Damian explained the duties of the margrave in terms of severe actions and paternal imagery. By contrast, in his letter to Adelaide, Damian used maternal imagery to praise Adelaide for her care for monasteries, whose monks were "secure under the shade of your protection, like featherless chicks warmed under maternal wings."[60] Moreover, Damian did not offer Adelaide historical rulers as a model. He could have used emperors or previous margraves[61] as exemplars, as he did with Godfrey, or female rulers, such as Adelaide's namesake, Empress Adelaide (ca. 931–999), grandmother of Otto III, or Galla Placidia (392–450), daughter of Theodosius. Instead, Damian urged Adelaide to imitate biblical heroines, particularly Deborah and Judith.[62] These were exemplars of strong women, who were apt in several ways. Deborah was unique among Old Testament heroines in holding an office which gave her legitimate authority. "She 'presided as judge over the people, and the Israelites went up to her for justice' [Judges 4:4–5]. Following her example, you [Adelaide] too govern your land without a man's help, and those who wish to settle their disputes flock to you for your legal decision."[63] Equally, Damian cites the example of Judith, a chaste widow, who was frequently presented as a figure for medieval queens and noblewomen to follow.[64] In particular Damian refers to Judith and the priest Ozias (Judith 8:12–13) to emphasize that there were times when a woman could legitimately exercise authority over men.[65]

Although these exemplars are apt, they are also highly gendered. Michael Gledhill argues that Damian "takes a different tack" in his letter to Adelaide from his approach to other laywomen.[66] Yet, to a large extent, Damian followed the same gendered paradigms when writing to Adelaide that he used with other laywomen. Biblical heroines are common to all of Damian's letters to laywomen, but not to laymen.[67] Moreover, the biblical stories of Deborah and Judith depend on the opposition of male and female and the reversal of traditional gender roles. Deborah and Jael's triumph over Sisera (Judges 4), and Judith's defeat of Holofernes (Judith 8–16), hinge on the imbalance of power between them. Their stories rely on what Megan McLaughlin has termed "gender paradoxes": the idea that the power of God is so great that it can overturn the "natural order" of gender relations and allow even a woman to triumph.[68] With his reference to the victory of these biblical heroines, Damian implicitly utilized gender paradoxes to make the same point. He also used this trope explicitly. Damian argued that it was not surprising that God saw fit to grant Adelaide, "his unworthy servant, some small degree of power over men, since at times he endows even a despicable plant with wonderful qualities."[69] Damian never describes Godfrey in this way. Damian's use of gender paradoxes accepts and reinforces traditional stereotypes regarding women and power. He also utilized other well-known medieval tropes when describing Adelaide's authority. It is often argued that in the Middle Ages the qualities of "masculinity" and "femininity" were not binary opposites, but part of a continuum.[70] A high-status woman could thus be gendered "male" in connection with her authority over others. Damian addressed his letter to "Duke Adelaide"[71] and praised her for being a woman in whom "virile strength reigns in a feminine breast."[72] Yet for Damian, this gender continuum went only one way. He praised certain women for their "manly" behavior,[73] but rarely rebuked men for "womanly" behavior. In particular, Damian did not accuse Godfrey of acting effeminately when he failed to conform to Damian's ideals of secular masculinity. Instead he warned Godfrey against behaving like a priest.

Damian's use of gender paradoxes and his references to "Duke" Adelaide and her "virile strength" suggest that, for him, male power was the norm and that partaking of masculinity, if only metaphorically, was a prerequisite for female rule. This is further underlined by his description of Adelaide—and the biblical heroines he offered her as models—as "virago[s] of the Lord."[74] Damian uses the term "virago" only twice in his letters: first in relation to Adelaide; and second in connection with Godfrey's wife, Beatrice, who is also the only other woman whom he addresses with a masculine title. He calls Beatrice "a most excellent duke and courageous virago" because of her support for the church.[75] In Damian's conception viragos were worthy of admiration for their "manly" strength, their actions on behalf of the church and, significantly, for their personal chastity.

Many medieval writers linked chastity with female effectiveness in spheres traditionally reserved for men.[76] The reasons for this were partly for etymological,[77] but an underlying, if often unacknowledged, reason was that it ensured that powerful women did not become models for subversive female behavior. Moreover, it made it easier for a celibate hermit, such as Damian, to have dealings with laywomen. Although the equation of chastity with good rulership was long-standing, it took on greater resonance in a letter in which Damian was urging Adelaide to enforce clerical celibacy.

Adelaide was a widow in her forties when Damian wrote to her. Damian urged her not to marry again, but to preserve her "lily-white chastity."[78] He also stressed the chastity of the biblical heroines he offered her as models. Judith, for example, was the model of "a widow's continence."[79] According to Damian, the enemies of these biblical heroines were defeated not simply by the women's strength, but also by their virtue: Sisera, "the leader of lust" (*luxuria dux*) was slain by "the sharp blade of chastity" (*mucro pudicitiae*).[80] Again, this emphasis is Damian's: as he acknowledges in the next paragraph, Jael actually drove a tent-peg (*clavus tabernaculi*) into Sisera's head.[81] This violent imagery stands in contrast with Damian's earlier admonition to Adelaide to be merciful, and instead recalls his advice to Godfrey to enforce discipline with severity. Significantly, however, Adelaide is not to use a tent-peg, nor yet the "prince's sword," but the "blade of chastity" to strike at her enemies.

While Damian undoubtedly thought that widows were spiritually superior to wives,[82] he did not urge Adelaide to remain chaste and unmarried for this reason, nor because he thought that he would have greater influence over her than any potential new husband. His emphasis on female chastity is not unique to his letter to the widowed Adelaide. Damian also stressed the chastity of biblical heroines in letters to married laywomen, and made it clear that such chastity was the precondition for their influence. Writing to Godfrey's wife, Beatrice, Damian explained that by living chastely, the biblical Sarah gained authority over her husband Abraham, so that he had to "'hearken to her voice' [Gen. 21:12]."[83] Damian used the same exemplar when writing to Guilla, wife of Margrave Rainer, to argue that when a wife exceeded her husband in virtue, she was permitted to have authority over him and he should "hearken to her voice."[84] Writing to Guilla, Damian also cited the example of Judith with the priest Ozias, which he had earlier used in his letter to Adelaide, to emphasize there were times when a woman could have authority over men.[85] Both for Adelaide and these other laywomen, Damian argues that it was only by being chaste and pious herself that a woman could legitimately exercise authority over others. By contrast, as Damian mentions in several letters, Godfrey was also chaste[86] yet this virtue was, at best, incidental to his rule. At worst, it actually undermined him: as we have seen, Damian warned Godfrey against blurring the lines between secular and priestly status. To be a good margrave Adelaide had to exercise self-control, but Godfrey had to control and dominate others.

Conclusion

Scholars who have previously discussed Damian's letter to Adelaide have often seen it as evidence that Damian dealt with female rulers in the same way as male ones. Comparing Damian's letters to Adelaide and Godfrey indicates that Damian does attribute certain characteristics to them that are not gendered: both Adelaide and Godfrey were to protect the poor and be generous to monasteries. Yet contrasting these letters indicates that Damian also made clear, and gendered, distinctions between Godfrey and Adelaide. As with his other correspondents, Damian offered them models which were appropriate to their status and which were also in accord, as far as possible, with socially accepted gender roles. Damian thought that certain models and characteristics were more appropriate for male margraves than female ones. These different models indicate that Damian conceived of Adelaide's rule differently from Godfrey's. Their location and behavior played a role in this, but Damian offered Godfrey and Adelaide different models primarily because of their gender.

Damian's conception of Godfrey's rule is more straightforward, and rigid, than his view of Adelaide's rule. Although there was a religious dimension to his activities, Godfrey was primarily to confine himself to administering secular justice and not become involved in religious punishments, as he had done at Ancona. Damian saw a clear distinction between secular and priestly masculinity, and urged Godfrey to conform to ideals of aristocratic manhood. He was to act with paternal and imperial authority; to use violence and severity to enforce discipline; and to "cut down evildoers" with the "prince's sword."

Like Godfrey, Adelaide was a strong and determined ruler and Damian acknowledged her status. Juxtaposing these letters in fact demonstrates, more clearly than has previously been recognized, that for Damian Adelaide was in many ways a more successful margrave than Godfrey. He certainly envisaged her as having a wider sphere of influence: Damian wanted Adelaide to intervene not only in priestly, but episcopal, matters and enforce clerical celibacy. In regard to clerical wrongdoing, she was to emulate biblical heroines from the Old Testament, to act with "virile strength," and to use the "blade of chastity" to enforce discipline.

Yet Damian also utilized many of the same gendered models for Adelaide that he used when writing to other laywomen. In relation to the administration of justice he urged Adelaide to behave mercifully with evildoers and have maternal care for monasteries. By contrast, Damian never told Godfrey to act with mercy. In this respect, Damian wrote to Adelaide as though she was the wife of a ruler, rather than a margrave herself. Damian tried to "solve" the problem produced by a female margrave by adapting suitable models for laywomen—whom Damian saw in nurturing, intercessory and above all, ancillary, roles—and incorporating these into the public and political role required of a margrave. The tensions between these models suggest that, for Damian, creating a mirror for a female margrave was more complicated than for a male margrave.

Acknowledgments

I am grateful to the organizers of the Gender and Medieval Studies Conference and to participants for comments on my paper. Thanks also to Kay Creber, Jinty Nelson, Serena Ferente, Michael Gledhill, Penny Nash, and Hanna Kilpi for reading earlier drafts, and special thanks to Elena Woodacre and Katherine Weikert.

Alison Creber is a graduate student at King's College, London.

Notes

1. Damian's letters are edited by Kurt Reindel, *Die Briefe des Petrus Damiani*, MGH Briefe d. dt. Kaizerzeit 4, 4 vols. (Munich: 1983–1993) (hereafter Reindel). English translation by Owen J. Blum and Irven M. Resnick, *The Letters of Peter Damian*, 6 vols. (Washington, DC: Catholic University of America Press, 1989–2005) (hereafter Blum).

2. Nicholangelo d'Acunto, *I laici nella Chiesa e nella società secondo Pier Damiani: ceti dominanti e riforma ecclesiastica nel secolo XI* (Rome: Istituto storico italiano per il Medio Evo, 1999), 305–330, 353–360; Michael Gledhill, "Peter Damian and 'the World': Asceticism, Reform and Society in Eleventh-Century Italy" (PhD diss., King's College, London, 2012), chapter 2.
3. Joan M. Ferrante, *To the Glory of Her Sex: Women's Roles in the Composition of Medieval Texts* (Bloomington: Indiana University Press, 1997), 14–17; Gledhill, "Damian," 117–126.
4. Ferrante, *Glory,* esp. 66.
5. For an overview: Reindel, "Einleitung," in Reindel 1: 1–32, esp. 1–13; Blum, "Introduction," in Blum 1: 3–33.
6. Letters 67 and 68. Damian also wrote two further letters to Godfrey: Letters 148 and 154.
7. Letter 114.
8. On Godfrey: Rudolf Jung, *Herzog Gottfried der Bärtige unter Heinrich IV* (Marburg: Elwert Verlag, 1884).
9. On Adelaide: Giuseppe Sergi, *I confini del potere: Marche e signorie fra due regni medievali* (Turin: Einaudi, 1995), esp. chs. 3–5.
10. Also called "mirrors for margraves"; see Nicholangelo d'Acunto, "L'aristocrazia del *Regnum Italiae* negli scritti di Pier Damiani," in *Formazione e strutture dei ceti dominanti nel medioevo. Marchesi, conti e visconti nel regno italico (secc. IX–XII),* ed. Amletto Spicciani (Rome: Istituto storico italiano per il Medio Evo, 2003), 336–337. The classic study is Hans Hubert Anton, *Fürstenspiegel und Herrscherethos in der Karolingerzeit* (Bonn: Bonner Historische Forschungen 32, 1968).
11. Letter 68: Reindel 2: 297; Blum 3: 87.
12. See, for example, Letter 68: Reindel 2: 291; Blum 3: 81. Letter 114: Reindel 3: 306; Blum 5: 304f.
13. Adelaide: Letter 114: Reindel 3: 296: *Adalaidi excellentissimae duci.* Godfrey: Letter 67: Reindel 2: 70; Blum 3: 70. Damian sometimes refers to Godfrey as "duke and margrave" or "margrave" in other letters: nos. 68, 140, 141, 148, 154.
14. Letters 67 and 68.
15. See, for example, Letter 67: Reindel 2: 283–284; Blum 3: 73.
16. Letter 67: Reindel 2: 286; Blum 3: 76.
17. Letter 68: Reindel 2: 292; Blum 3: 82.
18. Letter 67: Reindel 2: 283–284; Blum 3: 73.
19. Letter 114.
20. Letter 114: Reindel 3: 305–306; Blum 5: 304.
21. Godfrey's *placita*: Jung, *Gottfried,* Reg. nos. 5–11; Adelaide's *placita*: Domenico Carutti, *Regesta comitum Sabaudiae marchionum in Italia ab ultima stirpis origine ad anno MDCLIII* (Turin: Fratres Bocca, 1889), nos. CLX, CCIII.
22. See, for example, Berthold of Reichenau, *Chronicon,* in *Die Chroniken Bertholds von Reichenau und Bernolds von Konstanz, 1054–1100,* ed. Ian Stuart Robinson, MGH SS rer Germ NS 14 (Hannover: 2003), a.1069, 208–209; Bernold of Constance, *Chronicon,* in ibid., a.1069, 398; see d'Acunto, *Laici,* 305–313.
23. Jocundus, *Translatio sancti Servatii Tungrensis episcopi et miracula,* ed. Rudolf Koepke, MGH SS 12 (Hannover: 1856), ch. 56, 115.
24. Letter 60: Reindel 2: 204; Blum 2: 405; William D. McCready, *Odiosa sanctitas: St Peter Damian, Simony, and Reform* (Toronto: Pontifical Institute of Medieval Studies, 2011), 60–65.

25. For Godfrey as the prefect of Ancona, see *Chronicon sancti Huberti Andaginensis*, ed. Ludwig Bethmann and Wilhelm Wattenbach, MGH SS 8 (Hannover: 1848), ch. 23, 581. For Godfrey as the "one person," see Jung, *Gottfried*, 39–40; McCready, *Damian*, 64.
26. Letter 60: Reindel 2: 204; Blum 2: 405.
27. *Annales Altahenses maiores*, ed. Wilhelm Giesebrecht and Edmund von Oefele, MGH SS rer Germ 4, 2nd edition (Hannover, 1890), a. 1069, 78.
28. An exception is William of Chiusa, *Vita S. Benedicti II Abbatis Clusensis*, ed. Ludwig Bethmann, MGH SS 12 (Hannover, 1856), ch. 12, 205.
29. Letter 114: Reindel 3: 301; Blum 5: 299–300.
30. On Damian's Tuscan/Umbrian connections, see d'Acunto, "L'aristocrazia," 323–324; d'Acunto, *Laici*, 298–353.
31. On Damian's use of rhetoric, see Gledhill, "Damian," 53–62, 69–76.
32. On discipline and violence as crucial elements for aristocratic manhood, see Ruth Mazo Karras, *From Boys to Men: Formations of Masculinity in Late Medieval Europe* (Philadelphia: University of Pennsylvania Press, 2002), ch. 2.
33. Letter 67: Reindel 2: 285; Blum 3: 74.
34. See 2 Sam 1:1–15; Acts 5:1–11.
35. Letter 67: Reindel 2: 282–283; Blum 3: 72.
36. Letter 68: Reindel 2: 297; Blum 3: 87; Gledhill, "Damian," 112–113, 133.
37. Megan McLaughlin, "Secular and Spiritual Fatherhood in the Eleventh Century," in *Conflicted Identities and Multiple Masculinities: Men in the Medieval West*, ed. Jacqueline Murray (New York: Garland, 1999), 33–34.
38. Letter 68: Reindel 2: 290; Blum 3: 80.
39. Ibid.
40. Letter 68: Reindel 2: 292; Blum: 3 82; d'Acunto, *Laici*, 384–386.
41. Letter 67: Reindel 2: 286–288; Blum 3: 75–78.
42. Letter 67: Reindel 2: 288–289; Blum 3: 78.
43. Letter 68: Reindel 2: 292-297; Blum 3: 82–87.
44. Letter 67: Reindel 2: 288–289; Blum 3: 78.
45. Letter 110: Reindel 3: 243; Blum 5: 245; d'Acunto, *Laici*, 213–214.
46. Letter 67: Reindel 2: 286; Blum 3: 76.
47. Gledhill, "Damian," 101–105.
48. Letter 68: Reindel 2: 295; Blum 3: 84–85. On Hugh as a model for Godfrey, see d'Acunto, *Laici*, 316–319; Gledhill, "Damian," 108–112; McCready, *Damian*, 56–57.
49. Letter 68: Reindel 2: 293, 296–297; Blum 3: 83, 86.
50. Letter 68: Reindel 2: 292–293; Blum 3: 82–83.
51. Letter 67: Reindel 2: 281–282; Blum 3: 71.
52. Letter 67: Reindel 2: 281–282; Blum 3: 71; also Letter 68: Reindel 2: 293; Blum 3: 83.
53. d'Acunto, *Laici*, 309–310.
54. See Elke Goez, *Beatrix von Canossa und Tuszien: Eine Untersuchung zur Geschichte des 11. Jahrhunderts* (Sigmaringen: Jan Thorbecke Verlag, 1995).
55. Sharon Farmer, "Persuasive Voices: Clerical Images of Medieval Wives," *Speculum* 61, no. 3 (1986): 517–543.
56. Letter 51.
57. Letters 64 and 143.

58. Letter 112. D'Acunto, *Laici,* 356 argues that these letters are similar in content, but they actually provide further evidence that Damian wrote differently to men and women on the same subject: his letter to Cunibert emphasizes bishops' pastoral duty to their clerics; frequently cites canonical sources; and makes use of misogynistic and anti-matrimonial invective.
59. d'Acunto, *Laici,* 386–387.
60. Letter 114: Reindel 3: 301–302; Blum 5: 300. See also Matt. 23:37.
61. Damian was clearly aware of previous margraves of Turin: Letter 110: Reindel 3: 238; Blum 5: 241.
62. On biblical exemplars in Damian's letter to Adelaide, see Kimberly A. LoPrete, "Gendering Viragos: Medieval Perceptions of Powerful Women," in *Studies on Medieval and Early Modern Women 4: Victims or Viragos?* ed. Christine Meek and Catherine Lawless (Dublin: Four Courts Press, 2005), 30–31; Ferrante, *Glory,* 14–17.
63. Letter 114: Reindel 3: 297; Blum 5: 295.
64. Pauline Stafford, *Queens, Concubines and Dowagers: The King's Wife in the Early Middle Ages,* 2nd ed. (London: Leicester University Press, 1998), 26.
65. Letter 114: Reindel 3: 301; Blum 5: 298.
66. Gledhill, "Damian," 118.
67. On biblical figures in Damian's letters to laywomen, see Ferrante, *Glory,* esp. 16–17, 42, 56.
68. Megan McLaughlin, "Gender Paradox and the Otherness of God," *Gender & History* 3, no. 2 (1991): 147–159.
69. Letter 114: Reindel 3: 298; Blum, 5: 296; see also Reindel 3: 299; Blum 5, 297: "God at times uses women to achieve a more glorious triumph."
70. Carol J. Clover, "Regardless of Sex: Men, Women, and Power in Early Northern Europe," *Speculum* 68, no. 2 (1993): 377–378.
71. See note 13.
72. Letter 114: Reindel 3: 297: *cum virile robur femineo regnet in pectore*; LoPrete, "Viragos," 30–32.
73. See also Letter 64: Reindel 2: 226; Blum 3: 21; Letter 104: Reindel 3: 158; Blum 5: 162; Letter 136: Reindel 3: 466; Blum 6: 89; Gledhill, "Damian," 118.
74. Letter 114: Reindel 3: 299: *esto virago Domini.*
75. Letter 141: Reindel 3: 490: *Beatricis excellentissimae ducis et animosae viraginis.*
76. Ferrante, *Glory,* 14–18, 94–96, 113–114, 159–170; Ruth Mazo Karras, *Sexuality in Medieval Europe: Doing Unto Others* (New York: Routledge, 2005), ch. 2.
77. LoPrete, "Viragos," esp. 23–24.
78. Letter 114: Reindel 3: 304, 296; Blum 5: 303, 294.
79. Letter 114: Reindel 3: 300; Blum 5: 298.
80. Letter 114: Reindel 3: 299.
81. Ibid. See also Judges 4:21.
82. Ibid; d'Acunto, *Laici,* 357.
83. Letter 51: Reindel 2: 133; Blum 2: 336.
84. Letter 143: Reindel 3: 524–525; Blum 6: 147.
85. Letter 143: Reindel 3: 524; Blum 6: 146.
86. Letter 51: Reindel 2: 133; Blum 2: 336; Letter 68: Reindel 2: 290; Blum 3: 79; Letter 154: Reindel 4: 69; Blum 7: 73; d'Acunto, *Laici,* 311–312.

Chapter 2

Inaudito exemplo
The Abduction of Romsey's Abbess

Linda D. Brown

When Marie, the daughter of England's King Stephen and Queen Matilda of Boulogne, was oblated to God as a child, she became Christ's bride. Her new religious status as *sanctimonialis* veiled her with a nominal protection against sexual and marital predation. When she was later abducted by Matthew, the second son of Thierry, Count of Flanders, contemporary chroniclers in England and on the Continent reacted in different ways. Some included accounts and commentary about Marie's dramatic departure from Romsey Abbey in 1160, while others wholly ignored the event. Many of the former laid the blame at the feet of King Henry II of England for the unsavory deal he had struck with Matthew of Flanders. As far as Marie, the accounts—taken in isolation—almost exclusively portray her as an unwilling participant in the abduction.

This depiction can be seen in the account of Robert of Torigni, a monk of Mont Saint Michel, who explained how "Matthew the brother of the count of Flanders in an unheard of event led away the abbess of Romsey, who was the daughter of King Stephen, and with her seized the county of Boulogne."[1] Robert's choice of verbs, *duxit*, conveys the image of Matthew leading or drawing Marie away with him; his further use of *"inaudito exemplo"* compels the reader to imagine the abduction of an abbess as something that was an unheard of or unprecedented event. It was simply not done. Robert's tutting disapproval of the event is meek, however, in comparison with other commentators who introduce the notion of *raptus*. For example, three late twelfth- and early thirteenth-century annals and chronicles from the Low Countries emphasize the wickedness of the plot within the context of canon law: *"abbatisam raptam de monasterio," "de monasterio ubi erat Deo consecrata raptam,"* and *"contra fas legum … dedit uxorem [a Matheo]."*[2] Others supplement the account with accusations of viciousness, explaining that the marriage was effected *"per violentiam Regis Anglorum."*[3] Henry II was indeed well known for his strategies to arrange personally beneficial marital alliances in order to recoup his dwindling royal demesne.[4] That he would want to orchestrate and control a marriage for a family member of his rival is credible, particularly since Stephen's daughter had remained in England.

Rather than accepting the abduction narratives at face value, however, we must scrutinize them more critically to include the backstory and long-ranging consequences. As for the role to assign Marie, she can be read more fully within the context of family and personal history and the cultural, social, and political environment in which she lived. This exercise in extrapolation inevitably leads us back to the centrality of status, especially but not exclusively in regard to Marie herself. In order to situate her more convincingly and fully in the narrative, my research relies on a range of historical sources, including cartulary, epistolary, charter, and sigillographic material. These sources yield a striking number of labels and titles for Marie and signpost the changes that marked her life. Marie, like her counterparts in the mid-twelfth century, experienced a range of identities as she developed from child and daughter to mature woman. Although many of the labels were ordinary and predictable, others were not only unconventional but also controversial. The main purpose of this paper then is to decipher the former through an understanding of the latter, and to view their clashing juxtapositions with regard to Marie's gender and status.

Filia Regis Stephani Anglorum

It is generally assumed that Marie was born to Queen Matilda and King Stephen in Blois in the late 1120s or early 1130s. Marie's royal birthright influenced her most consistently applied descriptor: the daughter of Stephen, King of England. She self-identified in this style and temporarily as the Countess of Boulogne in the extant, *sigillographic* records that originate with her: one letter, two deeds, and their two attached seals. Regardless of the outcome of her father's reign as the usurper of the English throne, Marie never relinquished this identity. Her mother, Queen Matilda of Boulogne, left a legacy as the woman who played a pivotal role in protecting her family throughout the war and leaving her mark on swathes of land through her patronage in Boulogne and in England.

Marie was one of five children born to Stephen and Matilda, although only Marie and her brothers Eustace and William survived infancy. For a twelfth-century royal daughter, we might expect little written contemporary evidence apart from a smattering of chronicle entries registering her birth or a summation of her role at a particular religious house. Such is not the case for Marie and, although often confusing and even contradictory, a range of material does survive and provides coverage of her life from early childhood until death. Likewise Marie could have appeared in the records as a mere footnote in more modern scholarship, obscured by the events of the day and by her elder siblings, but scholars over the centuries have taken a keen interest in her life. The scandal in part accounts for such interest.

Pueritia habitu religionis initiate

Marie's family life was disrupted—to say the least—by the civil war and uncertainty of the period, and the *Genealogia Comitum Flandriae* tells us that she was from childhood admitted into the religious habit.[5] We cannot say definitively that this choice was influenced by the war; given that Stephen and Matilda were enthusiastic patrons of monasticism, it was not extraordinary that they should pledge their daughter to God. We must assume that their intention was for Marie's religious vow to be a permanent one until death. While child oblation was far from being a fixed process by the mid-twelfth century, it had sufficiently evolved to disallow a departure later in life without sufficient grounds. Marie's future positions of authority within religion furthermore would have sealed her status as firmly avowed.

The first written evidence linking Marie to a religious house comes from Brittany at the monastery of Saint Sulpice-la-Forêt, established by one of Robert Arbrisel's disciples as a house for both monks and nuns.[6] Its cartulary names her as the abbess, but assigns unworkable dates for these assertions.[7] Although undoubtedly problematic, an association between Marie and this Breton house did exist in various ways. The first of these links came in the late 1140s when Marie and companions from Saint Sulpice entered the English Benedictine house at Stratford-at-Bow or more correctly into St. Leonard's Priory in Middlesex.[8] Political and military changes might have prompted the decision to bring the young Marie to England. Most particularly, the death of Robert of Gloucester in 1147 had signaled a lull in fighting and a general change in the war between King Stephen and Empress Matilda. Marie and the Breton nuns did not remain long at Stratford, however. Discontent arose as a result of what they perceived as Stratford's onerously strict rule.[9] Marie's parents intervened to calm the situation, as evidenced by a charter of the Archbishop of Canterbury, Theobald.[10] Possibly as early as 1148, Theobald confirmed the establishment of a new religious house in Kent.

Prioressa

Marie is generally noted as the prioress of this new house, Lillechurch Priory. Queen Matilda's itinerary likely influenced the choice of locations, as she was temporarily living in Canterbury, overseeing construction of the family mausoleum in Faversham.[11] Despite the priory's hurried creation, Lillechurch quickly became financially stable and successful. In addition to endowments made by Marie's two brothers, Lillechurch made money via the ferry service it controlled between Kent and Essex. Although Marie stayed at Lillechurch for some six years, her family suffered great loss beginning in 1152 when Queen Matilda died at Castle Hedingham in Essex.

Her burial at Faversham Abbey was followed within the next two years by the death of the family's son and heir, Eustace, and then of the king himself. Thus, by late 1154, only Marie and her brother William survived. Despite such loss and upheaval, William was not in an undesirable position. His marriage to the heiress, Isabel de Warenne, had brought him land and prestige that were augmented when he assumed the comital title of Boulogne after Eustace's death. As for Marie, she too seemed well placed in her appointment as abbess at one of England's most prestigious houses. William and Marie were thus both installed in positions where a watchful king could hope to oversee and control them.

Abbatissa Romesia

Marie's promotion to the abbacy at Romsey Abbey occurred sometime after 1155, when the previous abbess died.[12] To explain the move to this ancient Wessex nunnery (founded in 907), Hampshire historian Judy Walker notes that its ambitious building plans likely prompted the search for a high-status abbess to solicit and support the funding needed for such a project.[13] Marie thus might have represented an ideal candidate, given her royal status, links to a powerful uncle, Henry of Blois, Bishop of Winchester and Abbot of Glastonbury, and experience in monastic administration.[14] By Domesday the prosperous nunnery at Romsey had boasted three mills in its two manors (*Infra* and *Extra*) and a rent sizeable enough to make it one of the twenty wealthiest monastic houses from the Anglo-Saxon period.[15] Marie, as its abbess, was in charge of administering these two manors. Since the 1140s, Romsey's abbesses had also received rents from twelve properties in Winchester.[16]

Despite such initial promise, Marie's time in Romsey was abbreviated by more family tragedy. Her brother William supported Henry II in his Toulouse campaign, waged in order to recoup lands claimed through Eleanor of Aquitaine. Ironically, William fought not only for his family's former adversary, Henry, but also against his former sister-in-law, Constance of France. Married to Eustace, and as such countess of Boulogne, Constance had left England after the deaths of Eustace in late 1153 and her father-in-law Stephen in 1154. She had returned to France and married Raymond V, count of Toulouse. Both Constance's and William's allegiances had been realigned as circumstances dictated. Consequently, William's childless marriage to Isabel and his death in October 1159 on return from the Toulouse campaign resulted in a void in Boulogne's leadership and a status-altering change for Marie. The impact of this shift set the wheels in motion for her abduction by Matthew of Flanders.

Rapta/Uxor

Confusion persists over why medieval writers described some events in terms of *raptus*. Inconsistently used, the noun and its related verbs were employed to convey multiple legal and social meanings.[17] Modern scholarship has thus wrestled to unlock its medieval usage and nuances. Caroline Dunn's recent book, *Stolen Women*, has categorized and defined the diverse vocabulary of rape and abduction.[18] Her work has similarly demonstrated how *raptus* was committed against both women and men. Recorded incidents range from the liberation of a daughter from an unsafe marriage to the abduction and rape of a woman by a known or unknown man.[19] As such, it is impossible to find consistency, even within a limited time period. *Raptus* might aptly describe Marie's departure from Romsey; conversely, the term might tell us more about the writers themselves and their own grievances—particularly against King Henry II.

Victorian historical biography depicted Marie as an abducted abbess cruelly torn from the bosom of religion and security.[20] Imagining her as a helpless victim does not sit comfortably, however, with what we know about her and her family. Although her subsequent marriage to Matthew was defined in terms of *raptus*, Marie's own role in agreeing to or even promoting the union cannot be discounted. As the daughter of Matilda of Boulogne, Marie had witnessed the importance of the county's rule. Queen Matilda had clearly nurtured this awareness in her children, and Eustace especially had directly benefitted from her acumen and experience.[21] As a result, family history might have taught Marie that assuming the comital title to Boulogne was the natural and correct option.

By the twelfth century, a nun, as the bride of Christ, professed perpetual vows of fidelity to her heavenly bridegroom. If she broke this vow for secular marriage, it was tantamount to adultery. Thus if Marie were seen as complicit in her abduction, she would have been branded apostate and excommunicate until returning to religion and undergoing penance. Likewise, deserting her vow would have cost her the prestigious position of abbess to which she had advanced. Nevertheless, lessons learned from Marie's family history would have taught her the value of choosing pragmatically and ambitiously when confronted by controversy and difficulty. Not only had Stephen usurped the throne, undoing his oaths to the Empress Matilda, but so too had Eustace gone his own way after the agreements between the Plantagenets and his father. Queen Matilda, no stranger to meeting the unpredictable with practical, no-nonsense solutions, had frequently proven her abilities for maverick and brave actions. For Marie, then, it was perhaps the combination of filial duty, family pride, and the potential for self-aggrandizement and advancement that justified the abandonment of her religious status.

Outspoken opponents of the abduction and marriage included the then-chancellor Thomas Becket. Chroniclers such as Herbert of Bosham and Matthew Paris reported the future archbishop's disapproval.[22] This seems to be more than a post-dated veneration of a future saint, as Thomas's opposition resulted in a long-standing and well-documented feud with Matthew of Flanders in years to come. The marriage also purportedly outraged Matthew's own family. As punishment for the secret scheme—that is, the marriage arrangements to which they were not privy—Matthew's father and brother stripped him of the castle in Lens that should have formed part of his new lands.[23] Charter evidence indicates, however, that the breach was speedily resolved. By 1161, Matthew was back in the family fold. One of Thierry's charters dated from the following year not only contains Matthew as one of its witnesses but also describes him alongside Philip as one of his sons.[24]

Clerical indignation in the locality of Boulogne similarly erupted for Matthew, at least for a time. His reported disregard for ecclesiastical authority resulted in at least two separate promulgations of excommunication against him and an interdiction for the people of Boulogne.[25] Marie is not named in either of these excommunication orders. Over time, local tensions subsided and tempers calmed, especially as Matthew and Marie proved to be generous benefactors to ecclesiastical and monastic projects.[26] The one person unwilling to forgive and forget, however, was the one who mattered most: Pope Alexander III. He did not accept the marriage and worked over the course of nine years to dissolve it. By 1168, the Pope launched a successful attack when he backed a dubious dower claim on behalf of Constance of France.[27] Her marriage to Raymond of Toulouse had ended in the mid-1160s in a bitter and pathetic repudiation; Alexander III then used Constance's claim to dower as leverage against Marie and Matthew. Alexander's letters make clear his intention of using Constance's dower—*concessum in dotalitium*—to force them out of Boulogne.[28] He threatens excommunication for the count *and countess* and another interdiction in the county, if they did not comply—that is, leave—within three months. Significantly, this is the first instance of Marie's inclusion in the threat of excommunication.[29]

Comitissa Boloniensi

At about this same time, Marie wrote her own letter, the one extant example from her correspondence. It underscores her status within northern European politics, her continuing animosity for Henry II, and her attempt to curry favor with a man of papal influence: Louis VII. As the King of France, Louis was indeed influential with Alexander III and, significantly, he was also Constance's brother. Reading like an intelligence memo, Marie's letter states:

> Let it be known ... that Henry, king of England, has sent his ambassadors to the emperor ... The returning ambassadors passed through my territories, and I spoke with them, and well I perceived from their words that the English king ceases not, day nor night, to devise mischief against you. Wherefore I thought it fitting to ... give you the necessary forewarning, that you may take counsel with your wise men, and act as is most fitting, lest the impetuous presumption of the fraudulent king should inflict violent injury upon you.[30]

This letter was likely sent with several objectives: to show good will toward Constance's brother at the time of the dower challenge; to demonstrate solidarity for Alexander's papacy against competition from Victor IV, whose greatest supporter was the Emperor Frederick I himself; and to enact a small degree of revenge against the man on the English throne. For Marie, Henry II remained little more than a pretender. For us, it reveals a woman searching for allies, and clearly in the habit of receiving emissaries who passed through her county.

Marie's words may indeed have influenced how the drama of the dower claim ended. By 1170, the finishing touches to an elaborate compromise were completed. The terms were complex: the marriage dissolved, Marie was to return to the religious life; Matthew was to keep the title of count through his daughters; the daughters were to be legitimized by the pope; and he, Alexander III, was to put the house where Marie would retire under his protection. As far as Constance and her dower claim were concerned, apparently nothing was accomplished. She did not return to Boulogne.[31]

Sanctimonialis

After some quick rearranging of financial and familial matters, Marie entered the nearby Royal Abbey of Sainte-Austreberthe in Montreuil. Life's dramas did not come to an abrupt halt at its gates, however. Between her resumption of the holy habit and her death, she continued to lead an active life, including the possibility of another encounter with Thomas Becket. Perhaps corroborating a warm friendship or a healed wound, Thomas wrote a nun, ca. May 1170. The letter from "Archbishop Thomas of Canterbury to his Beloved Daughter Idonea" communicates the need for an envoy to thwart the coronation of Henry the Younger in York. The nun's instruction is to "hand over the Lord Pope's letter ... to our venerable brother, Roger, archbishop of York, if possible in the presence of some of our brothers and fellow-bishops; or ... in the presence of those who happen to be there."[32] Professor Anne Duggan suggests that the nun "Idonea" to whom he is writing is in fact Marie. Her supposition is based partially upon the mission's promised reward, that is "the remission of your sins, an imperishable reward, and the crown of glory, which the blessed sinners Magdalene and the Egyptian finally received from the Lord Christ, when all the stains of their former lives were totally expunged."[33] Duggan footnotes her belief about Marie as a possible candidate, which she asserts "may be a pseudonym for Mary of Blois, only recently returned to the religious life."[34] John of Salisbury also wrote about this letter, which "had long crossed the sea" before 14 June 1170.[35] If Marie was indeed "Idonea," her need to cross the Channel to deliver the letter as well as her need for penitential acts could explain the identity of the letter's recipient. In the name, Idonea, we may furthermore perceive the diminutive form of the family name, Ida.[36]

At Marie's new house of Sainte-Austreberthe in Montreuil, she remained busy and apparently attracted attention as a leader, as evidenced by later commentators mistakenly referring to her as abbess.[37] True to form, she continued to ratify charters for Matthew. Additionally, she helped facilitate matters with the monastery of Saint-Josse for the nearby construction of Matthew's new chateau.[38] This new build would be significantly closer to Marie in Montreuil than to Boulogne. The sources are divided about the next phase of Matthew's personal life. Some medieval writers, such as Gislebert de Mons, write that he married Eleanor de Vermandois, the sister of his sister-in-law, Isabelle.[39] What is certain is that both Matthew and his brother, Count Philip, were no friends of Henry II by this point. Matthew, in support of Henry the Younger, was killed by a crossbow bolt in 1173. The loss was especially acute for Philip, who is said to have abandoned the fight and gone home.[40] The relationship between the two brothers had been strong, and it appears that potentially the same can be said of Matthew's relationship with Marie. In a charter of donation made in the year of his death, Matthew had clearly referred to Marie as *uxor mea* (my wife). No linguistic qualifiers such as "*quondam*" (formerly) are used.[41] These word choices and Marie's later establishing of prayers for Matthew's soul suggest that the couple still considered themselves married. The care and attention lavished on Matthew's tomb further support this conjecture.[42]

With Matthew's death, Marie became effectively widowed, regardless of the couple's previous marital dissolution. Once again she responded to family needs and, with or without papal approval, she left the nunnery to care for her daughters and "*pour achever leur éducation.*"[43] Once the girls were married—probably 1177—Marie returned to Sainte-Austreberthe. At this point, she established obits for her former husband and herself.[44]

Filia regis Stephani

Of Marie's death in 1182 we know very little. One medieval obituary draws together the rich collection of identities and changes of status that mark her life: "Marie the daughter of Stephen, the King of England, formerly the abbess of Romsey in England, afterwards the wife of Matthew, the Count of Boulogne, resumed the holy habit in the house of Montreuil."[45] An additional note describes, "some of her gifts to the nuns are controlled by them even now."[46] Such largesse can be seen in the charter evidence of the divorce settlement, in which Marie provided ten *livres* for the clothing of nuns.[47] Further corroboration of her generosity comes from two undated charters regarding land donations to Lillechurch Priory. The deeds not only document her provision of land to the priory but also underscore her relationships with other religious women. One of the witness lists includes seven men of various secular and religious positions and three nuns: "et sanctimonialibus, Juliana, Ereburga, and Ermelina, & multis aliis."[48] Not unique but certainly rare, this inclusion of nuns may convey Marie's own desire to incorporate women alongside men in the official business of the everyday. Both charters acknowledge, "*Ego Maria Regis Stephani Anglie.*"[49]

The three seals attached to these two charters provide more information about Marie and the priory. Careful examination of the two damaged seals reveals that Marie's own seal is attached to both deeds. Their worn inscriptions inform the viewer that they belong to the daughter of the English king. Standing and dressed in a flowing gown and veiled, Marie holds a book in

Illustration 2.1 Grant to Lillechurch Priory. St. John's College, Cambridge D46.27. Reproduced with kind permission of the College Council, St. John's College, Cambridge.

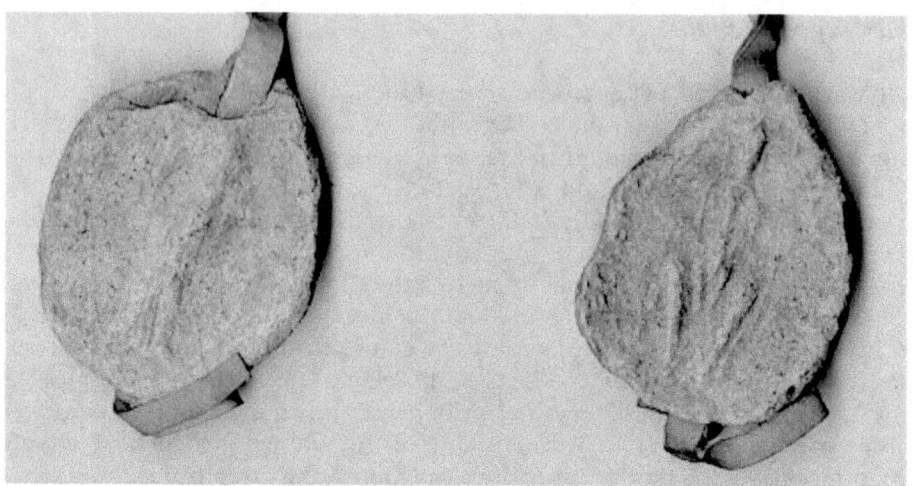

Illustration 2.2 Grant to Lillechurch Priory. St. John's College, Cambridge D46.58. Reproduced with kind permission of the College Council, St. John's College, Cambridge.

her left hand and flower or bird in her right, as her uncovered left foot steps forward. As for the third seal, it answers a centuries-old mystery. The *Monasticon Anglicanum* notes that Lillechurch Priory's seal has not been discovered.[50] This seal, however, is most certainly that priory's seal. More damaged than Marie's, it depicts the seated Virgin and Child enthroned, in recognition of the priory's dedication to St. Mary. From the faint inscription, eight of the twelve letters of *Lillecherche* can be discerned along the seal's left side.

Family lineage, memory, and memorialization remained important to Marie's descendants. Daughter Ida, one year after her mother's death and ten years after her father's, "made concessions to the abbey of Licques concerning a tithe at Westaxla 'for the soul of her father and her mother'."[51] Ida's husband, Renaud Dammartin, remembered the weal of the souls of "Mathieu, Count of Boulogne and Marie, his wife" in a grant of free passage ca. 1200.[52] In family commemorations, Marie and Matthew remained resolutely married.

Conclusions

Despite confusion about the nature or even existence of a *raptus* in 1160, Marie's marriage to Matthew of Flanders was directly tied to the status and gender of both abductee and abductor. Had Marie not become the family heiress, it is unlikely that the second son of the Count of Flanders would have chosen an abbess for his wife. For her, the greatest shift in status occurred when her brother William died. Overnight she became the last member of her natal family and heiress to its lands, fortune, and responsibilities. Undoubtedly an attractive target for marriage brokers, Marie may too have seen herself in a new light. She now possessed the means, obligation, and motivation to assume her familial role as countess of Boulogne. At a stroke, her status shifted from religious leader to secular leader, and she crossed a divide not generally allowed at the time. Taking into account the possibility of abduction does not clarify matters as to her willingness or resistance in that crossing over, just as the inclusion of *raptus* by some chroniclers does nothing to clarify the actual departure from Romsey. What can be more confidently stated is that numerous opportunities existed in the early months of her marriage to escape, if this had been her desire. The marriage was not secret, and local churchmen, English political leaders like Chancellor Thomas Becket, and the Pope himself opposed the union and could have facilitated Marie's return to Romsey or elsewhere. Yet the marriage lasted some nine years.

Marie and Matthew's union can be regarded as successful in a number of ways. The marriage produced two heirs, ensuring a stable transition of comital power in future. Their eldest daughter, Ida, served as countess after Marie's return to the nunnery until she died in 1216, when her daughter, Matilda III, assumed the leadership. Under Marie and Matthew, the county itself benefitted from strong governance and direct, on-site leadership. Neither of Marie's two brothers would have provided this sustained contact with Boulogne, diverted as they were by more pressing English affairs. During Marie and Matthew's nine years, the county's churches and monastic houses profited from their patronage, mirroring the largesse shown by Marie's parents on both sides of the Channel.

The multiple changes in status that Marie experienced were simultaneously enhanced and limited by gender. Being a female religious theoretically did not liberate or constrain her any differently than her male counterparts. However, monastic reformers had argued for greater security and stricter enclosure for nuns. As a secular woman, Marie realized uniquely female life experiences. She gave birth to two daughters, lived with Matthew as his wife, and later became effectively his widow. Her later exploits regarding her daughters' care provide a fuller view of Marie as a mother. Regardless of whatever label and status were ascribed to Marie at a particular time, she did not frivolously push at boundaries but instead acted conservatively and pragmatically. In the end, evidence portrays Stephen and Matilda's daughter using her lineage, status, wealth, and skills to effect progress even as she ensured that continuity was preserved.

Acknowledgments

My thanks to Drs. Kathy Krause and Heather J. Tanner for their support in forming our panel, "Gender and the Traces of Authority," for the Gender & Medieval Studies conference at the University of Winchester, and for their continuing encouragement of my research.

Linda D. Brown is Academic Developer at Anglia Ruskin University.

Notes

1. Robert de Monte, "Chronica," in *Patrologiae Cursus Completus (Anno 1216)*, ed. Jacques-Paul Migne (Paris: Garnier, 1880), 160: 492. "Matheus filius comitis Flandrie inaudito exemplo duxit abbatissam Rummesia, que fuerat filia Stephani Regis, et cepit cum ea comitatum Boloniensem."
2. *Monumenta Germaniae Historica Scriptores* (Impensis Bibliopolii Aulici Hahniani: Hanover 1826), 6:490, 397, and 404. These excerpts read as "the kidnapped abbess from the monastery," "snatched from the monastery where she was consecrated to God," and "against the divine law of laws given as wife to Matthew."
3. "By violence of the English king." Ibid., 1:409.
4. Some contemporary chroniclers, particularly those with links to Henry II, completely ignored the event. This group includes Roger of Hoveden, Roger of Wendover, and the continuator to Florence of Worcester's chronicle.
5. An appendum to *Genealogia Comitum Flandriae*, in *Monumenta Germaniae Historica*, ed. George Henry Pertz (Hanover: Impensis Bibliopolii Hahniani, 1851), 326.
6. Bruce L. Venarde, *Women's Monasticism and Medieval Society: Nunneries in France and England, 890–1215* (Ithaca: Cornell University Press, 1997), 65.
7. Denis de Sainte-Marthe and Barthélemy Hauréau, *Gallia Christiana: in provincias ecclesiasticas distributa* (Paris: Didot, 1856), 14:787.
8. William Dugdale et al., *Monasticon Anglicanum* (London: Longman, Hurst, Rees, Orme & Brown [etc.], 1817), 6:378–382. David Knowles, and R. Neville Hadcock, *Medieval Religious Houses England and Wales* (London: Longman, 1971), 255.
9. Dugdale, *Monasticon Anglicanum*, 4:381.
10. Dugdale, *Monasticon Anglicanum*, 4:381; William Page, ed., *The Victoria County History of Kent* (London, 1926), 2:145–146. Avrom Saltman, *Theobald Archbishop of Canterbury* (London: Athlone Press, 1956), 379–380 provides a transcription of the transaction. The sisters of Stratford were obliged to release the manor Lillechurch, initially given to support the royal daughter.
11. Richard Eales, "Local Loyalties in Norman England: Kent in Stephen's Reign," in *Anglo-Norman Studies VIII: Proceedings of the Battle Conference, 1985*, ed. R. A. Brown (Woodbridge: Boydell Press, 1986), 105. Travel along the modern A2, an ancient road connecting the north of the county to the port at Dover, would have seen mother and daughter within a day's journey of one another.
12. Henry Richards Luard, ed., *Annales Monastici* (London: Longman, Green, Longman, Roberts, and Green, 1864), 2:55.
13. Judy Walker, *Romsey Abbey through the Centuries* ([Romsey]: Romsey Abbey, 1999), Appendix 5, xvii.
14. Opinions vary concerning the building works at Romsey. In 1872, Reverend Edward Berthon attributed to Marie "the chief part, and the completion of the Romanesque portion" of the abbey church. A century later, architectural historian, M. F. Hearn, noted how Marie's departure "can only have interrupted all but the most basic activities in the nunnery and probably accounts for the awkward cessation of work on the fragmentary nave for another two decades." In 2001 however, archaeologist Ian R. Scott supported an "early twelfth-century date for

the start of the work on the Norman abbey ... on stylistic grounds." *The Architect: A Weekly Illustrated Journal of Art, Civil Engineering, and Building*, 8 (1872): 78; M. F. Hearn, "Romsey Abbey: A Progenitor of the English National Tradition in Architecture," *Gesta* 14 (1975): 40; Ian R. Scott, "Romsey Abbey: Benedictine Nunnery and Parish Church," in *Monastic Archaeology: Papers on the Study of Medieval Monasteries*, ed. Graham Keevill, Michael Aston, and Teresa Anne Hall (Oxford: Oxbow, 2001), 150.
15. Janet Burton, *Monastic and Religious Orders in Britain* (Cambridge: Cambridge University Press, 1994), 9.
16. Frank Barlow et al., *Winchester in the Early Middle Ages: An Edition and Discussion of the Winton Domesday* (Oxford: Clarendon Press, 1976), 356. The modest rents can be traced in the records to the decade before Marie's arrival.
17. *Raptus* might variously describe abduction, rape, or even rescue. Caroline Dunn, *Stolen Women in Medieval England: Rape, Abduction, and Adultery, 1100–1500* (Cambridge: Cambridge University Press, 2013).
18. Dunn examines the permutations of language involving such words as *raptus, rapere, rapuit, abducere,* and *abduxit. Stolen Women*, 18–51.
19. Ibid., 20–21.
20. Such a portrayal is seen in Mary Anne Everett Green, *Lives of the Princesses of England from the Norman Conquest* (London: Longman, Brown, Green, Longman & Roberts, 1857), 1:192–214.
21. Charters from 1147–1152 demonstrate Eustace witnessing, confirming, and making grants as the count of Boulogne; C. Johnson, H. A. Cronne and R. H. C. Davis, *Regesta Regum Anglo-Normannorum*, (Oxford: Clarendon Press, 1968), 3: nos. 24, 195–196, 222, 229a, 239c, 551, and 847.
22. James Craigie Robertson, *Materials for the History of Thomas Becket Archbishop of Canterbury* (London: Longman & Co 1877), 3:328. Matthew Paris, *Historia Anglorum*, ed. Sir Frederic Madden, Rolls Series (London, 1906), 1:315–316.
23. The confiscation of the Castle at Lens may have been an empty gesture to demonstrate Thierry's disapproval of the uncanonical marriage. The castle had and continued to play an important role for both Boulogne and Flanders. It was eventually returned to Boulogne.
24. Archives Départementales Lilles, 10H 43/697.
25. The initial excommunication apparently resulted from his scandalous marriage to Marie. The second was meted out for Matthew's mistreatment of clergy in Boulogne when he found secular clergy willing to sidestep the interdiction, ejecting the former who were following it. Martin Bouquet, *Recueil des historiens des Gaules et de la France* (Paris: L'Imprimerie Impériale, 1808), 15:788.
26. For example, donations to churches and abbeys in Saint Ulmar, Clairmarais, and Samer undoubtedly mended more local fences. See Étienne Baluze, *Histoire Généalogique de la maison d'Auvergne: justifiee par chartres, titres, histoires anciennes et autres preuves authentiques* (Paris: Antoine Dezallier, 1698), 137–138.
27. Bouquet, *Recueil*, 15:866–867, letters CCXXXI and CCXXXII.
28. Bouquet, *Recueil*, 15:867, letter CCXXXII.
29. Many antiquarian and modern scholars, however, have tended to include Marie when discussing the previous orders of excommunication.
30. Bouquet, *Recueil*, 16:144. For a translation of the entire letter see Mary Anne Everett Wood Green, *Letters of Royal and Illustrious Ladies of Great Britain* (London: Henry Colburn, 1846) 1:11–13.

31. After seeking refuge with her brother, Louis VII, and giving birth to a son (with whom she was pregnant at the time of the repudiation), Constance spent time in the Holy Land. Visible in various land transactions, she eventually took vows as a *consoror* with the Hospital of Saint John in Jerusalem. Laurent Macé, *Les Comtes de Toulouse et leurs entourage, XIIe–XIIIe siècles: rivalités, alliances et jeux de pouvoir* (Paris: Privat, 2003), 62–63.
32. Saint Thomas Becket, *The Correspondence of Thomas Becket, Archbishop of Canterbury, 1162–1170,* ed. Anne Duggan (Oxford: Clarendon Press, 2000), 1234–1235.
33. Ibid.
34. Ibid., fn 1, 1234.
35. Ibid., fn 7, 1235.
36. Marie's great-grandmother, (possible) great-aunt, and elder daughter shared the name. See H. Tanner, *Families, Friends and Allies: Boulogne and Politics in Northern France and England, c. 879–1160,* Northern World, Vol. 6 (Leiden: Brill, 2004), 290–291.
37. Ibid.
38. Auguste Braquehay, *Essai historique sur l'Abbaye Royale de Sainte-Austreberte à Montreuil-sur-Mer* (Abbeville: Imprimerie du Cabinet Historique de L'Artois et de la Picardie, 1895), 23.
39. L. Napran, *Chronicle of Hainaut* (Woodbridge: Boydell Press, 2005), 53.
40. *Roger of Wendover's Flowers of History: Comprising the History of England from the Descent of the Saxons to A.D. 1235,* trans. J. A. Giles (London: H. G. Bohn, 1849), 24.
41. Baluze, *Histoire généalogique,* 2:97–98.
42. The tomb is now exhibited at the Musée de Boulogne-sur-Mer. Made of black Belgian marble, it depicts Matthew as a mail-covered knight in repose with two beautiful dogs at his feet and towers and angels at his head.
43. "To complete their upbringing"; Henri Malo, *Un grand feudataire, Renaud de Dammartin et la coalition de Bouvines* (Paris: H. Champion, 1898), 14.
44. *L'Abbaye Royale de Sainte-Austreberte à Montreuil-sur-Mer,* 23.
45. *Gallia Christiana,* 10:1319: "filia Stephani Angliae regis, quondam abbatissa Ronvesii [*sic*] in Anglia, postea uxor Matthaei comitis Boloniensis, [et] habitum sanctimonialis apud Monstrolium resumsit."
46. Ibid.: "nonnulla monialibus largita, quibus etiamnum potiuntur."
47. François Ganneron, "Les Comtes de Boulogne, Manuscrit de 1640," in *Commentaires et notes par F. A. Lefebvre* (Boulogne-sur-Mer, 1891), 178.
48. "And the nuns Juliana, Ereburga, and Ermelina, and many others." Grant to Lillechurch Priory, St. John's College, Cambridge, D46.27.
49. D46.27 writes the identification in full, while D46.58 abbreviates it.
50. *Monasticon Anglicanum,* 4:381. Judith Everard identifies this seal as Lillechurch Priory's, providing a detailed description of it in her article, "The Abbey of Saint-Sulpice-La-Forêt and Royal Patronage in England, c. 1150–1257," *Nottingham Medieval Studies,* 2003, 47:141 Appendix 1.
51. Erin L. Jordan, "The 'Abduction' of Ida of Boulogne: Assessing Women's Agency in Thirteenth-Century France," *French Historical Studies* 30, no. 1 (2007): 11.
52. Grant to the Abbey of La Trinité in Fécamp, 48433:GB 133 BMC/78, c. 1200. John Rylands Library, Manchester University.

Chapter 3

The Corpus Christi Devotion
Gender, Liturgy, and Authority among Dominican Nuns in Castile in the Middle Ages

Mercedes Pérez Vidal

The feast of Corpus Christi was established in 1264 by Urban IV; however, because the feast made little headway in popular imaginations, being adopted by only a few isolated churches, it had to be refounded in 1311 by Clement V and in 1317 by John XXII, who added the festival to the papal ceremonial, developing the octave, the Eucharist exposition, and the solemn procession.[1] This last ritual became the most characteristic element of the feast, as well as an outstanding and lavish civic ritual. It not only survived but was even reinforced after Trent, as a result of the definition of Transubstantiation in 1551 by the Council.[2] Indeed, the solemn procession, bearing the Host through the city, was gradually interpolated with pageants and plays (*autos*), as well as dances, and all these elements gained importance during the Baroque period.

In the Iberian Peninsula, the first Corpus Christi celebrations date from the beginning of the fourteenth century. In the crown of Aragon, the Corpus was celebrated in Barcelona in 1319, whereas in Castile the earliest documented procession took place in Toledo at least since 1333.[3] Curiously, in both

Aragon and Castile, the first known depictions of the Corpus Christi procession belonged to female nunneries and were located in the nuns' choir. For example, the altarpiece of the Cistercian nunnery of Vallbona de les Monges (1349–1350), and in Toledo, in the base of the so-called *Virgen del Pajarito*, made in the fifteenth century and preserved in the Dominican nunnery of Santo Domingo el Real.[4] In both of these nunneries, the foundresses and prioresses belonged to the aristocracy and many were closely connected with royalty. In Toledo, three prioresses were related to King Pedro I: Teresa de Ayala, with whom the king had a daughter, María de Castilla—who also became a prioress—and Catalina de Castilla, granddaughter of the same king.[5]

Despite the increasing interest in female monasticism in Spain, only a few studies have adopted a gender approach in the analysis of liturgy and religious images and in the functionality of art and architecture. The particular case of the Corpus Christi festival reflects this lack of attention. Nevertheless, this feast and devotional practice had great importance in the empowering of these aristocratic women, not only through the commission of works of art, but also through the liturgical performance and the use of monastic spaces. However, all these were also highly contested areas between the nuns and male clerics and friars, and women did not always succeed in their ambitions for shaping their own spaces.

Illustration 3.1 Corpus Christi procession in the base of the "Virgen del Pajarito," in the nuns' choir of Santo Domingo el Real de Toledo (fifteenth century). Photo: M. Pérez Vidal.

The Role of Dominicans in the Origin of Corpus Christi Devotion

The veneration of the Eucharist by Saint Francis and Saint Clare is well known, whereas—probably as a consequence of the Order of Preachers' disregard for their own liturgical history—the key role played by the Dominicans in the institution of the Corpus Christi festival has frequently been forgotten.[6] However, Juliana of Liége, whose visions are purported to have been the origin of the festival, consulted with Dominicans as well as other religious for advice regarding her vision. One of the Dominicans she consulted was Hugh of Saint-Cher, at the time provincial of the Order of Preachers in France, and later Vicar General of the Order and Cardinal-Legate. He approved the idea of the new feast of Corpus Christi in 1240, presented it to the bishop of Cambrai, and strongly supported the initiative both among the official hierarchy of the church and the laity by preaching and granting of indulgences.

The composition of the office, adopted by the General Chapter of 1324, was attributed to Aquinas by Pierre-Marie Gy, noting that the idea of a corporeal presence in the Eucharist was used neither in this office nor in other works by Aquinas.[7] Subsequent studies of Zawille showed that the inspiration of the office's *historia* was in the *Postilla*, or biblical commentaries, of Hugh of Saint-Cher, who could consequently also be considered its composer.[8]

Although the Corpus Christi feast was incorporated into the Dominican liturgy only in 1304, in some provinces it was celebrated earlier.[9] Moreover, we also have early evidence of the opening of windows in the rood screen (*tramezzo*) to see the Holy Sacrament. According to Galvanno Fiamma, the choir of San Eustorgio of Milan, built in 1239, had already two "windows" through which friars could see the host.[10] The full visibility of the main altar to the congregation became a necessity from the twelfth century onward, but this was reinforced as a result of the complete adoption of the doctrine of transubstantiation at the 1215 Fourth Lateran Council.[11] The direct consequence of this shift in emphasis was the adoption of some architectonic solutions, such as retrochoirs, elevated choirs at the western end of the nave, or even the location of lay people in the transept.[12]

In the case of Dominican nuns and other religious women, devotion to the Eucharist was even more emphatic, becoming almost an obsession, probably as a reaction to other limitations imposed on them, that even were in contradiction with the aforementioned need to see the host and reveal the altar.[13] Indeed, from the ninth century onwards, councils and collections of canon law tried to limit and withdraw women from the lay people and clergy and also from the Eucharist celebration; this trend reached its culmination during the twelfth century, as can be seen in the *Decretum Gratiani*. The priesthood became the sole means of mediating the divine presence and the women were dismissed as ritual agents as they could not administer communion or touch the vessels; women even received communion less frequently, whereas priests took it daily.[14] Moreover, there was an increasing interest on imposing a more strict enclosure on nuns. All these prohibitions were reiterated in the subsequent councils and treatises of the thirteenth century.[15] A consequence of all this was the adoption of barriers, screens, and other devices shielding the altar; as a result, the Eucharist was usually not visible from the nun's choir, as has been studied in the case of the earlier nunneries of the Poor Clares in Italy.[16] Thus, this was in clear contradiction with the need to see the Holy Sacrament, reinforced as a result of the Fourth Lateran Council.

Overcoming Women's Limitations

Both nuns and some patronesses quickly evolved ways to overcome these limitations. We have early evidence of Dominican nuns in Castile requiring the ability to see the Corpus Christi, even earlier than the well-known examples from the Poor Clares. In the nunnery of Santa María de las Dueñas of Zamora, apart from the already-blessed host, which was preserved in the choir, the record of a pastoral visit in 1279 informs us that some nuns felt a driving need to gaze upon the altar in the church where the Corpus Christi was preserved.[17] Similarly, Dominican nuns of Caleruega were authorized in at least 1288 by Munio de Zamora—but probably before by King Alfonso X— to open the grills of the choir in the most important festivities to see the Corpus Christi.[18] Similar openings, located upon the altar of the choir, were documented in other nunneries: in Santo Domingo el Real de Madrid *sobre el altar de las dueñas*, although in this case we have later testimonies.[19]

The fourteenth century brought about changes and new ideas concerning liturgical participation for women. They were allowed to take communion only a few times a year but the importance of having a view of the altar—and the host placed upon it—was emphasized. This was reflected in female saints' hagiographies and nuns' lives, in which descriptions of viewing the host were common. In some of them, religious women even received the chalice to give communion.[20]

However, women empowered with the aforementioned privileges regarding the Eucharist frequently belonged only to the aristocracy or royalty, and some of them promoted the Corpus Christi devotion in their foundations.[21] Berenguela de Anglesola y Pinós, prioress of Vallbona de les Monges (1348–1377), founded a chapel devoted to the Corpus Christi in the nuns' choir, commissioning the altarpiece and also a panel.[22] In the same way, the Eucharistic devotion of Queen Sancia of Majorca was reflected not only in the primary dedication of Santa Chiara of Naples to the *Corpus Domini*, but especially in the building of a retrochoir to the east.[23]

What happened in the Dominican convents and nunneries? We must bear in mind the theological differences between Dominicans and Franciscans. Whereas the latter supported the cult of the blood and the host and related Eucharist miracles, following Duns Scotus, Dominicans—but also the majority of theologians, including many Franciscans—followed Thomas Aquinas, who stated that the "substance," that is to say the real presence of Christ, was unseeable. Thus the view of flesh, blood, or a Christ Child was a construction of the beholder, not a real presence.[24]

Probably as a result of these theological arguments, Eucharistic miracles were not frequently depicted in Dominican altarpieces. We find some exceptions, however, such as the altarpiece of Tamarite de Litera, made between 1340 and 1360, and one of the first Spanish cycles dedicated to Saint Dominic of Guzmán, which might have been influenced by stories circulating concerning the miracle of the mule of Saint Antonio di Padua.[25] This was also the case of the tomb of San Raymond of Peñafort in the cathedral of Barcelona.[26] In any case, both of these examples, as well as the aforementioned of Vallbona de les Monges, must be understood in the political context of the Crown of Aragon, where the Eucharist was strongly promoted, but we do not find parallels in Castile.

Reform, Counterreformation, and Subtle Resistance

Although Dominicans were frequently very passionate in their sermons and the Dominican women's lives included frequent descriptions of great intensity, the Order apparently tried to control and avoid excesses in artistic depictions, particularly between the end of the fourteenth and the beginning of the sixteenth century. Nuns did not easily accept male impositions, however, and they developed ways of empowerment through artistic production and liturgical celebration. The *Schwesterbuch from Töß*, written around 1340 by Elsbeth Stagel and copied and illuminated a hundred years later in the nunnery of St Katherine of Nuremberg, reflects this subtle "independence" of nuns. This book included images in which the nuns assumed male roles, touching the Child like the priest touches the host.[27]

Curiously, at the same time, Tommasso Caffarini emphasized the zeal of Saint Catherine of Siena in taking communion in his additions to the *Legenda Maior* of Raimondo de Capua, recounting how she left the impression of her teeth while biting the sacred vessels. He also emphasized the miracle of the host.[28] Illuminations also exist from the same century that depict these amazing episodes, such as Saint Catherine touching and drinking from Christ's wound.[29] Nevertheless, in many cases reformers tried to avoid or suppress these kinds of images, especially in mural paintings and altarpieces, as women were not allowed to touch or even to be near the Corpus Christi. We find a striking example in the refectory of San Domenico di Pisa, where the fresco of Benozzo Gozzoli's workshop depicting the crucifixion was modified by painting several friars between some Dominican nuns and the central group as mediators.[30]

Crucifixions were common in the decoration of refectories, whereas depictions of the Last Supper apparently became popular only after the Council of Trent. Nevertheless, in some cases even before Trent, nuns' refectories were decorated with a scene of the Life of Saint Dominic, which can be seen as a reenactment of the Last Supper: the miracle of the loaves. The version of Blessed Cecilia, written between 1277 and 1288, located the miracle in Rome, and among the details she mentioned was the preservation of the remains of the miraculous bread and wine by the nuns of Santa Maria in Tempulo. This was clearly linked both with the memory of the founder and the establishment of the Order but also with the Eucharist, as Saint Dominic was clearly depicted as *"alter Christus."*[31] We find this scene in the wall of the infirmary refectory—*grasso o delle bisognose*—of Saint Niccolò di Prato.[32]

The nuns of Santo Domingo de Madrid also had relics related to both the Eucharist and Saint Dominic. They preserved for centuries the corporals, the chalice, and a portable altar in which Saint Dominic celebrated mass, as well as a fragment of bone, another of his cape, a leaf from his prayer book containing some words from the Saint Agatha office, the chain with which he made penance, and the letter addressed to the nuns in 1220.[33]

Nuns in Procession

A curious processional banner is preserved from San Domenico di Pisa, depicting Christ wearing priest's robes and holding a large chalice in his left hand, as if he was offering communion to the Dominican nuns. This banner was carried in the Corpus Christi procession in substitution of the host.[34] Although it is supposed that nuns' processions took place without the Eucharist being present, because nuns could not handle the host,[35] this was not always observed. Hildegard von Bingen had already considered the possibility of women's access to the priesthood—although not to the office of the altar—following the example of the Virgin, as she compared the Conception and Incarnation of Christ with the transubstantiation of the Corpus Christi by the priest.[36] During the Middle Ages and even in the early modern period, after Trent, it was not unusual for abbesses and prioresses to be in charge of worship and liturgy in their respective monasteries, even wearing the priestly vestments, as seen for instance in the chair of Santa María de Sigena's prioress, made for the princess Blanca de Aragon y de Anjou (1321–1347), in which she was depicted carrying the *gremiale* (the cloth bishops drape over their laps during rituals of the mass).[37] Moreover, they donated, commissioned, and even wrote liturgical books; in some cases they had an outstanding role in the liturgical performance of their nunneries and even beyond their monastic walls. Constanza de Castilla, prioress of Santo Domingo el Real de Madrid and granddaughter of Pedro I, wrote a personal book of prayers that was also used by the nuns in their communal liturgy. The work was focused once again on the Passion and Incarnation of Christ, thus closely linked with the devotion to the Corpus Christi, and she described these episodes with expressive and sensual images.[38]

In some cases prioresses also carried the monstrance and led processions, such as the one celebrating the feast of the Corpus Christi. Some of these processions were inside the cloisters and likely with the participation of some friars or male clerics, such as in Santo Domingo de Caleruega.[39] But prioresses could also lead processions outside the enclosure walls, as the prioress of the Dominican nuns of Toledo did.[40]

Contravening Romans' Disposition: The Corpus Christi Inside the Enclosure

Although processional monstrances from Dominican nunneries in Castile have not survived for the period before the Baroque, we have a medieval *ciborium* from San Juan Bautista de Quejana. This piece, made in Venice between the first quarter of the fourteenth century and the beginning of the fifteenth, was probably donated to the nunnery by Fernán Pérez de Ayala, the grandson of the founder.[41]

Moreover, the frontal and altarpiece originally located here, in the Chapel of the Virgen del Cabello, and now preserved in the Chicago Art Institute, has been considered a commission of Leonor of Guzmán, the Chancellor's wife, and probably made by a local workshop, as evidenced by its style.[42] The repetition of the Adoration of the Shepherds and the Adoration of the Magi on the frontal was probably not a mistake but done purposely, as in other groups of frontals and altarpieces.[43] The central area of the lower register of the altarpiece has an empty throne presided over by a star, and the

Illustration 3.2 San Juan Bautista de Quejana, Chapel of the Virgen del Cabello: copy made by Cristóbal González de Quesada in 1959 of the Retable and Frontal of the Life of Christ and the Virgin, now at the Chicago Art Institute. Photo: M. Pérez Vidal.

Wise Men in the nearby scene suggest the probable presence of an image of the Virgin here, or maybe the same reliquary that gave name to this chapel. However, as Tormo suggested, it could have also been topped, at least in some occasions and alternating with the aforementioned reliquary, by the Eucharistic *ciborium* donated by the grandson of the founder. Supporting this hypothesis is the fact that the Adoration of the Magi had a clear Eucharistic meaning.[44] If this were true, we have an example of conservation of the Blessed Sacrament outside the altar of the church, in a nearby chapel, contravening the requirements of Humbert of Romans, according to whom the sacrament must be preserved in the main altar of the church.[45]

These spaces are better known in Poor Clare nunneries. Nevertheless, apart from the chapel of Quejana, we find other spaces with the same functions in Dominican nunneries in Castile from the fourteenth century onward, although these have not been well studied. These spaces were frequently designed as lateral choirs—usually coexisting with other choirs located at the western end of the nave, or elevated choirs—and were located near the presbytery, near or above the sacristy, and also near the dormitory. They were often used for night prayers, for ill and elderly nuns, or for penance, gaining indulgences, and the adoration of the Corpus Christi, although this was not always present. They frequently also contained an image of the Virgin. We find these spaces in Caleruega, Toro, and Salamanca. The use of these spaces continued after the Council of Trent; moreover, some of them were made in the wake of the Council, like the *corito* (lateral choir) of Santo Domingo el Real de Toledo.[46]

In the antechoir of Santo Domingo de Segovia, also located in a lateral space and near the cemetery, we find a fragment of an altarpiece with the

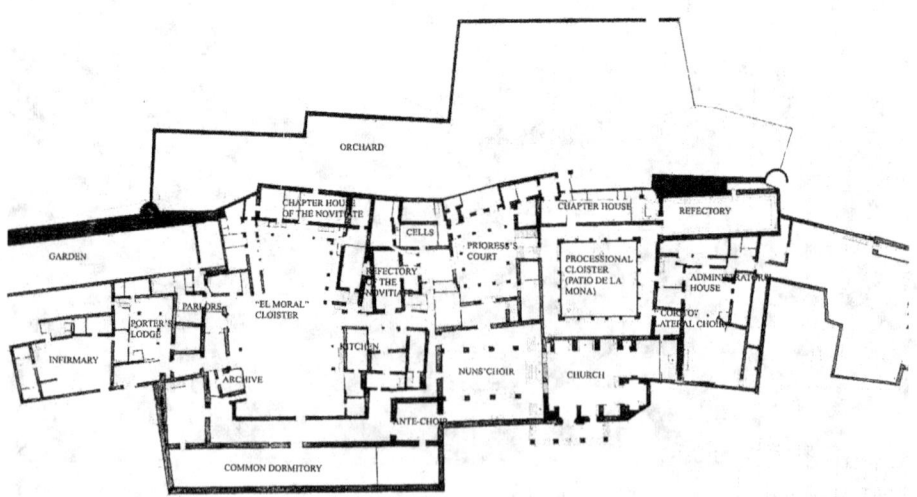

Illustration 3.3 Santo Domingo el Real de Toledo at the end of the sixteenth century. Author's reconstruction.

Mass of Saint Gregory dating from the fifteenth century. Although it was subsequently also associated with the Transubstantiation, this iconography was initially closely linked to penance and frequently to a funerary context.[47]

In other cases we do not find a complete depiction of this theme but only the Man of Sorrows or the *Arma Christi,* also with a clear penitential and Eucharistic meaning. Thus we can see how Dominican nuns, following Saint Catherine of Siena, persisted in their devotion to the blood of Christ, despite the aforementioned opposition of Aquinas. We find these dramatic depictions in the cloister of el Moral Santo Domingo de Toledo, made at the beginning of the sixteenth century, probably because of the Beata de Piedrahita, a reformer clearly influenced by Savonarola, who followed the example of Saint Catherine. In this same nunnery also existed a depiction of the Communion of the Virgin, which was an iconographic theme that became popular after Trent. This depiction is unfortunately lost but known thanks to a photo preserved at the Archivo Histórico Provincial of Toledo.[48] This image could serve as a model for the religious at the time of receiving the *Viaticum,* and thus it was probably located in the infirmary. The iconography regarding the Corpus was indeed omnipresent in Santo Domingo el Real de Toledo, as a reflection of the local outstanding performances, but probably also as choice of these aristocratic women.

Corpus Christi in the Nuns' Choir

As we have already seen, in some cases the Corpus Christi was preserved in a different place from the main altar. This is well known in the case of the houses of the Poor Clares, and also Cistercian nunneries. We have similar examples in the case of some Dominican nunneries. For instance, the Blessed Sacrament was preserved in the main altar of the choir of Unterlinden at least since the first half of the fourteenth century and friars entered the nuns' choir during certain festivals.[49] In Santo Domingo el Real de Toledo, according to the testament of Inés de Ayala, dated 1398, the Sacrament was also likely preserved in the nuns' choir. This happened also in Sancti Spiritus de Benavente. In other cases, although its location is not clear, we have evidence of the existence of an altar dedicated to the Corpus Christi in Santo Domingo el Real de Madrid—at least since 1375—and in Santa Catalina de Ávila y San Miguel de Trujillo.[50]

In the wake of the Council of Trent, Councils and treatises forbade the preservation of the Corpus Christi in a different place from the main altar of the church, such as the aforementioned synod of Toledo in 1582.[51] Nevertheless, Tridentine prescriptions were frequently ignored; for example, the Dominican nuns of Salamanca and Medina del Campo still preserved the Corpus Christi in their choir at the end of the seventeenth century.[52]

In the same way, chapels dedicated both to the Holy Sacrament and Our Lady are documented in the Dominican nunneries of Lekeitio and Bilbao.

A stranger case, a "chapel of *comunión*" or "house of communion" was located in the wall between the choir and the church in Madre de Dios of Toledo, and also decorated with an altar devoted to Our Lady.[53]

Conclusions

Dominican nuns in Castile also had an active role in the creation and performance of liturgy and devotions, in which the Corpus Christi occupied a central place. As we have seen, particular features of this devotion considered hitherto specific of the Poor Clares or Cistercian nunneries can also be traced in Dominican foundations. Thus, the creation and performance of liturgy seem to have been caused more by the gender and social status of nuns than by belonging to one Order or another. Despite the reformers' attempts to deprive nuns of their independence, some aristocratic women found subtle ways of subversion. They defined the religious practices, the artistic production that decorated their churches, the use of monastic spaces, and they not only recreated the urban processions inside the cloister but also transgressed, in some cases, the enclosure boundaries themselves. By doing so, they overcame women's limited participation in the Eucharist as a way of reasserting their authority, social status, and self-government.

Mercedes Pérez Vidal was PISCOPIA-Marie Curie Fellow at the University of Padua, 2015–2017.

Notes

1. Miri Rubin, *Corpus Christi: The Eucharist in Late Medieval Culture* (Cambridge: Cambridge University Press, 1991), 184–185. The proceedings of the Conference at Orvieto in 2014, which focused on the Corpus Christi and commemorated the 750th anniversary of the papal bull *Transiturus* have been published: Agostino Paracivini Bagliani e Laura Andreani, *Il "Corpus Domini" Teologia, Antropologia e Politica,* SISMEL (Firenze: Edizioni dell Galluzzo, 2015).
2. *Canones, et Decreta Sacrosancti Oecumenici, et Generalis Concilii Tridentini sub Pavlo III, Iulio III, Pio IIII, Pontificibus Max: Index Dogmatum, et Reformationis* (Romae, Apud Paulum Manutium, Aldi F, 1564), XIII Session, chapter 4, f. 74.
3. Ramón Gonzálvez Ruiz, "El Corpus de Toledo en los siglos XIV y XV," *Memoria Ecclsiae* 20 (2002): 211–240.
4. Marisa Melero Moneo, "Eucaristía y polémica antisemita en el retablo y frontal de Vallbona de les Monges," *Locvs Amoenvs* 6 (2002–2003): 21–40; Palma Martínez-Burgos García, *Dominicas: VIII Centenario* (Toledo: Empresa pública Don Quijote de la Mancha, S. A., 2007), 198.
5. María Estela González de Fauve, Isabel Las Heras, and Patricia de Forteza, "Espacios de poder femenino en la Castilla bajomedieval: El caso del linaje de los Castilla," *Cuadernos de historia de España* 82 (2008): 99–122.

6. Juan Meseguer Fernández, "El culto a la Eucaristía en el Monasterio de Pedralbes Siglos XIV y XV," *Archivo Ibero-Americano* 157 (January–March 1980): 115–122; Caroline Bruzelius, "Hearing Is Believing: Clarissan Architecture, ca. 1213–1340," *Gesta* 31, no. 2 (1992): 85; Esther Wipfler, *"Corpus Christi" in Liturgia und Kunst der Zisterzienser in Mittelalter* (Münster: Lit. Verlag, 2003).
7. Pierre-Marie Gy, "L'Office du Corpus Christi et s. Thomas d'Aquin: État d'une recherché," *Revue des sciences philosophiques et théologiques* 64 (1980): 491–507.
8. Ronald Zawilla, "The Biblical Sources of the Historia Corporis Christi: Attributed to Thomas Aquinas: A Theological Study to Determine their Authenticity" (PhD diss., University of Toronto, 1985), passim.
9. The Corpus Office was made compulsory for the whole Order in the chapter of Florence of 1324 (*Monumenta Ordinis Fratrum Praedicatorum Historica*, IV, 3 and 128–129).
10. Gundisalvo Odetto, "La Cronaca Maggiore dell'ordine dominicano di Galvano Fiamma Frammenti Editi," *Archivum Fratrum Praedicatorum* 10 (1940): 292–373, esp. 326.
11. Vincent Lorne Kennedy, "The Moment of Consecration and the Elevation of the Host," *Mediaeval Studies* 6 (1944): 121–140.
12. Eduardo Carrero, "Presbiterio y coro en la catedral de Toledo: En busca de unas circunstancias," *Hortus Artium Medievalium* 15 (2009): 315–327.
13. Caroline W. Bynum, "Women Mystics and Eucharistic Devotion in the Thirteenth Century," *Women's Studies* 11, nos. 1–2 (1984): 179–214.
14. Gary Macy, "The Ordination of Women in the Early Middle Ages," *Theological Studies* 61, no. 3 (2000): 481–507, esp. 495; Anne Clark, "The Priesthood of the Virgin Mary: Gender Trouble in the Twelfth Century," *Journal of Feminist Studies in Religion* 118, no. 1 (2002): 11.
15. Gary Macy, *The Hidden History of Women's Ordination: Female Clergy in the Medieval West* (Oxford: Oxford University Press, 2008).
16. Bruzelius, "Hearing Is Believing," 83–91. However, other testimonies from Poor Clare nunneries, such as Ascoli Piceno, seem to suggest a possible visual participation of the nuns in the Eucharist, contrary to what Bruzelius pointed out. Emanuele Zappasodi, *Sorores reclusae: spazi di clausura e immagini dipinti in Umbria fra XIII e XIV secolo* (Florence: Mandragora, 2018), 18.
17. Peter Linehan, *The Ladies of Zamora* (Manchester: Manchester University Press, 1997), 48.
18. Eduardo Martínez, *Colección Diplomática del Real Convento de Santo Domingo de Caleruega con facsímiles de los documentos* (Vergara: Editorial de *El Santísimo Rosario*, 1931), 352.
19. Luis G. Alonso Getino, "Centenario y cartulario de nuestra comunidad," *Ciencia tomista* 20 (1919): 5–21; 129–152; 265–288, esp. 280.
20. Caroline W. Bynum, *Holy Feast and Holy Fast: The Religious Significance of Food to Medieval Women* (Berkeley: University of California Press, 1987), 13.
21. Dominique Rigaux, *A la table du Seigneur: l'Eucharistie chez les primitifs italiens, 1250–1497* (Paris: Cerf, 1989), 162.
22. Moneo, "Eucaristía y polémica antisemita," 21–40.
23. Caroline Bruzelius, "Queen Sancia of Mallorca and the Convent Church of Sta. Chiara in Naples," *Memoirs of the American Academy in Rome* 40 (1995): 69–100.
24. Antolín González Fuente, *Sacramentos, liturgia y teología en Santo Tomás de Aquino* (San Esteban: Salamanca, 2012), 143–182; Caroline W. Bynum, "Seeing and

Seeing Beyond: The Mass of St. Gregory in the Fifteenth Century," in *The Mind's Eye: Art and Theological Argument in the Middle Ages*, ed. Jeffrey F. Hamburger and Anne-Marie Bouchée (Princeton: Princeton University Press, 2006), 214–215.
25. Gemma Malé Miranda, "Nuevas aportaciones sobre el retablo de Santo Domingo de Tamarite de Litera: Iconografía, origen, promoción y datación," *Anuario del Departamento de Historia y Teoría del Arte* 20 (2008): 37–52, esp. 38.
26. Josep María Ainaud de Lasarte, "Un sant popular," in *Ramon de Penyafort i el dret català: quatre-cents anys de la canonització del patró dels advocats de Catalunya, 1601–2001* (Barcelona: Fundació Jaume I, 2000), 20–25.
27. Jane Carroll, "Subversive Obedience: Images of Spiritual Reform by and for Fifteenth-Century Nuns," in *Reassessing the Roles of Women as "Makers" of Medieval Art and Architecture*, ed. Therese Martin (Leiden: Brill, 2012), 703–737.
28. Silvia Nocentini, "Lo *scriptorium* di Tommaso Caffarini a Venezia," in *Hagiografica: Rivista di agiografia e biografia della Società Internazionale per lo studio del medioevo latino* (2005): 79–144.
29. Jeffrey Hamburger, "Un jardin de roses spirituel: Une vie enluminée de Catherine de Sienne," *Art de l'enluminure* 11 (2004): 2–75.
30. Anne Roberts, *Dominican Women and Renaissance Art: The Convent of San Domenico of Pisa* (Hampshire: Ashgate, 2008), 181–198.
31. Joanna Cannon, "Dominic *alter Christus*? Representations of the Founder in and after the Arca di San Domenico," in *Christ among the Medieval Dominicans: Representations of Christ in the Text and Images of the Order of Preachers*, ed. Kent Emery, Jr., and Joseph Wawrykow (Notre Dame, IN: University of Notre Dame Press, 1998), 35.
32. Silvestro Bardazzi and Eugenio Castellani, *S. Niccolò a Prato* (Prato: Cassa di risparmi e depositi di Prato, 1984), 269–273.
33. Gil González Dávila, *Teatro de las grandezas de la Villa de Madrid: Corte de los Reyes Católicos de España* (Madrid: Tomás Iunti, 1623), 276; Getino, "Centenario y cartulario," 14.
34. Roberts, *Dominican Women*, 157.
35. Rubin, *The Eucharist in Late*, 247.
36. Clark, "The Priesthood," 12–17.
37. Carmen Bernabé, "Silla prioral de Blanca de Aragón de Anjou," in *Maravillas de la España medieval: Tesoro sagrado y monarquía*, ed. Isidro G. Bango Torviso (Madrid: Junta de Castilla y León, 2001), 361–364.
38. Constanza de Castilla, *Book of Devotions-Libro de devociones y oficios*, ed. Constance L. Wilkins (Exeter: University Press, 1998).
39. Carmen González González, *Real monasterio de Santo Domingo de Caleruega: Fundación de Alfonso X El Sabio* (Salamanca: Editorial San Esteban, 1993), 163.
40. Elías Tormo y Monzó, "Informe acera de expediente sobre declaración de monumentos histórico-artísticos de las iglesias de San Justo y San Miguel y los conventos de Santo Domingo el Real y Capuchinas de Toledo," *Boletín de la Academia de Bellas Artes de San Fernando* 107 (1933): 108.
41. María Luisa Martín Ansón, "Una obra desconocida de la Tardía Escuela Veneciano Bizantina en el convento de San Juan de Quejana," *Reales Sitios* 146 (2000): 2–14.
42. Marisa Melero Moneo, "Retablo y frontal del convento de San Juan de Quejana," *Locus Amoenus* 5 (2000–2001): 33–51.

43. Victor M. Schmidt, "Ensembles of Painted Altarpieces and Frontals," in *The Altar and Its Environment* (1150–1400), ed. Justin. E. A. Kroesen, and Victor M. Schmidt (Turnhout: Brepols, 2009), 203–222.
44. Elías Tormo y Monzó, "Una Nota Bibliográfica . . . . y algo más: Acerca del Inventario Monuntal de Álava, y vergüenzas nacionales ante unos actos de impiedad histórica," *Boletín de la Sociedad Española de Excursiones* 24, no. 2 (1916): 152–160, esp. 156.
45. Humbert of Romans, *Opera de vita regulari*, vol. II, ed. J. J. Berthier (Rome, 1888–1889), 170.
46. Mercedes Pérez Vidal, "Estavan todas no coro e ben cantand' e Leendo. Tipologie e funzioni dei cori nei monasteri delle Domenicane dal XIII al XVI secolo, con particolare riferimento alla Castiglia," in *Spaces for Friars and Nuns: Mendicant Choirs and Church Interiors in Medieval and Early Modern Europe*, ed. Haude Morvan (Rome: École Française de Rome, 2021), 181–204, esp. 194–197.
47. Bynum, "Seeing and Seeing Beyond," 210.
48. Toledo, Archivo Histórico Provincial, Fondo Rodriguez, E-089.
49. Carola Jäggi, "Architecture et disposition liturgique des couvents féminis dans le Rhin supérieur aux XIIIe et XIVe siècles," in *Les dominicaines d'Unterlinden*, ed. Madeleine Blondel, Jeffrey F. Hamburger, and Catherine Leroy (Paris: Somogy éditions d'art, 2000), I:95.
50. Pérez Vidal, "Estavan todas no coro," 191.
51. Alfonso Rodríguez G. de Ceballos, "Liturgia y configuración del espacio en la arquitectura española y portuguesa a raíz del Concilio de Trento," *Anuario del Departamento de Historia y Teoría del Arte* 3 (1991): 43–52, esp. 45.
52. *Noticia de la fundación del Convento de Santa María de la Ciudad de Salamanca, Orden de Santo Domingo sacada de las historias que de dicha Orden escribió el Ilustrísimo y Reverendísimo Señor Obispo de Monopoli, 3 p. Cap 4. Esta la copia de la Escritura del Convento y Epitome de la vida admirable de Santa Ines de Montepulchiano, escrita por el V. P. M. F. Fernando del Castillo*, 2 p, cap. 32, 1698, Salamanca, Archivo de las Dueñas; *Relación del convento de Santa María la Real de las monjas de la ilustre villa de Medina del Campo de la Orden de Nuestro Glorioso Padre Santo Domingo por fray Gaspar de Alarcón, predicador General por esta provincia de España y confesor de dicho convento*, Rome, Archivum Generalium Ordinis Fratrum Praedicatorum, Serie XIV, Liber Q, Parte Seconda, ff. 1027–1045.
53. Juan López, *Tercera parte de la historia general de Sancto Domingo y de su Orden de Predicadores* (Valladolid: Francisco Fernández de Córdova, 1613; ed. facsimile, Valladolid: Maxtor, 2003), 283–284.

Chapter 4

From Villainous Letch and Sinful Outcast, to "Especially Beloved of God"
Complicating the Medieval Leper through Gender and Social Status

Christina Welch and Rohan Brown

In *Leprosy in Medieval England,* Carole Rawcliffe argued that leprosy was a disease that "played a notable part in the medieval imagination and was accorded significance far beyond the physical threat it actually posed to the population."[1] The unique hazard that leprosy represented can be seen through two unprecedented royal edicts, issued in 1346 and 1472, which were designed to remove lepers, initially from within the walls of London, but later from all major towns and cities.[2] The punishment for noncompliance with this edict, and for the crime of insidiously spreading the disease among the community, was that lepers were to be whipped as vagrant rogues, although there was also the threat of execution.

A literally rotten disease, there was no real cure for leprosy and no proper understanding of how this slow contagion spread. Furthermore, there was no real diagnosis and almost any skin condition could fall under the leprous label. Perhaps most significantly, during this period of history when there was no distinction between the social and the religious, lepers were a threat to both society and morality. Leprosy then can be understood as being more than a medical condition that affected real individuals. It was a socio-religious construct, and there was in the medieval mind-set a notion of the "ideal" leper: "ideal" in the Weberian sense of a non-real, utopian "accentuation of one of more points of view."[3] This "ideal" leper was a pedagogical symbol that represented both a social and moral status and was a figure in a physical and spiritual state of liminality, where bodily decay was a sign of moral corruption; and this "ideal" leper was male.

The notion that men were more prone to leprosy than women dates to the fifth-century Byzantine physician Aetius;[4] a finding reinforced in modern society by recent World Health Organization statistics which note that "although leprosy affects both sexes, in most parts of the world males are affected more frequently than females often in the ratio of 2:1."[5] Although women did contract leprosy in the medieval period, archaeological evidence suggests that it was a disease overwhelmingly associated with men. In the cemeteries of the leper hospitals of St James and St Mary Magdalene in Chichester, over 72 percent of all the leprous burials were male, and in Winchester and Buckingham on the whole the number of male skeletons outweigh those of females.[6]

We have chosen to explore the construct of the medieval ideal male leper by examining vernacular literature and medieval theology. We argue that, although the medieval leper was typically perceived of as an outcast experiencing a social death before succumbing to the slow degeneration of the disease, once explored specifically through the lens of gender and status, this image can be complicated, for in specific situations the leper was one of God's elect, destined for an afterlife that only the sainted enjoyed.

The Scientific Diagnosis of Leprosy and Its Social Effects

Ian Mortimer notes that in the Middle Ages, leprosy was the "most terrifying illness which people could imagine."[7] The most prolific and mutilating form known to contemporary medicine, *lepromatous leprosy*, is thought to have been a common medieval strain of the disease. Clinically this disease can take up to twenty years to fully manifest, initially presenting itself as nasal congestion, swelling of the limbs, and nerve damage. Eventually lesions manifest before ulceration of skin and eyeballs occurs; nodules emerge and the extremities would become paralyzed and eventually rot away. Mortimer claims that lepers would have suffered from alopecia, bodily bleeding, putrefaction of the nose and penis, as well as loss of teeth; considering these symptoms, one must concur with his view that "ultimately lepers were wholly deformed, stinking, repulsive and blind … [and] that is why it was called the 'living death'."[8]

The description of the Summoner's affliction in Chaucer's *Canterbury Tales* provides a useful view of perceptions of the contagion. Typically a lower-class church official who "brought people before the ecclesiastical court for acts such as illicit intercourse,"[9] as Walter Curry notes, "Chaucer's Summoner is dangerously ill, suffering from a species of morphea known as *gutta rosacea*, which has already been allowed to develop into that kind of leprosy called alopecia, according to the medieval understanding of his symptoms."[10] This could be indicated by the Summoner's "fire-red face ... the details about the eyebrows, his narrow eyes, and the white 'whelkes' and 'knobbes' on his cheeks,"[11] although whether he in fact had scabies is a moot point, for medieval medical doctors grouped skin conditions together. In the *Science of Surgery* by the thirteenth-century doctor Lanfrank, it is noted that "lepers will have other common signs," meaning that if someone had leprosy they also had scabies.[12]

Many scholars, such as Michael Foucault,[13] Saul Brody,[14] and Bryan Turner,[15] consider that by the end of the twelfth century, the subject of leprosy was so prolific in vernacular literature that one could easily construct an image of a veritable leprous epidemic. Though leprosy was by no means a "new" disease, such as the plagues that were to follow in the fourteenth century, the demographic of those infected with leprosy suddenly altered during the twelfth century. From 1100 to 1175, leprosy infected "large quantities among the dispossessed, leaving its former victims [the elite, wealthy, nobles and bishops] alone,"[16] and with this social change in the spread of the disease, aspects of social control also altered. With, as Johan Goudsblom notes, "the rich and powerful seem[ingly] ... practically immune" to the condition,[17] and with the alteration to socio-economic conditions resulting in masses of landless poor and destitute individuals, there was a certain practicality in labeling vagabonds, beggars, and even heretics as lepers. Jeremy Seabrook elucidates that as the "threat" from religious justifications for disturbances to the social order receded, "'the poor' [were seen] as a secular menace to society [who] accompanied the dissolution of Feudalism. Migratory, unattached, begging, the mass of poor were enfranchised from Feudalism."[18] This in turn provoked resentment within society, representing the decay of order.[19] The decline of feudalism was accompanied by new interpretations of Christian doctrine, particularly texts such as the *Festial* of the English Augustinian Canon Regular, John Mirk, which insisted on compassion for the poor, the oppressed, and the sick.[20]

As accusations of leprosy rose, so did the need for segregation, for while leprous individuals were a physical threat to society, they also represented society's depravity, and both needed containing. Further, both the body and soul needed treating, and this was achieved through the construction of *leprosaria*: a form of hospital, built outside of city perimeters and incorporating a cemetery and often a chapel with a priest, which accommodated the physical and spiritual care of the leprous patient. Large towns and cities typically had numerous *leprosaria*, and overall, there were approximately three hundred constructed in England before the early fourteenth century, demonstrating the rising rates of supposed infection during this time period.[21] It should be noted, however, that although these hospitals were integrated into the social fabric of medieval society, they contained fewer lepers than one might imagine.

Sexuality and Leprosy: A Medieval Calculus

The typical medieval male leper was understood as lusty and carnal; the edit of 1346 in England stated that infection was by "way of mutual communication ... as by carnal intercourse with women in stews."[22] This notion was represented in vernacular culture in characters such as the sex-crazed lepers in Shakespeare's *Troilus and Cressida*[23] and the lepers in the medieval romance *Tristan and Isolde,* who suggest that the adulterous Isolde be handed over to them to be raped to death.[24]

For women, too, it should be noted that there was a strong association between leprosy and sex. Aetius had suggested leprosy was contractable via sexual contact,[25] as did the Abbess Hildegard of Bingen (1099–1179), who believed it was firmly associated with lustful sex;[26] a suggestion posited by the first century Greek physician Aretaios.[27] Meanwhile, some medieval commentators asserted the condition was contracted through having sex with menstruating women;[28] thus a further link between leprosy and improper sexual conduct.

Lepers' exaggerated physical deformity, and the physical pain that accompanied it until their eventual deaths, did not promote sympathy to the medieval onlooker. Rather, the fact that the disease progressed slowly and could be concealed during the early and most infectious stages provoked accusation within the community, with the accusations necessitating a target suspect. The manifestation of the disease itself provided some indication as to why victims were infected; in particular, the decomposition of the nose demonstrated a direct link to leprous contagion and sexual misbehavior. In medieval society loss of the nose "was widely regarded as a sign of infamy, since it served to brand criminals and sexual miscreants."[29] Such an obvious deformity could not be hidden and unequivocally highlighted that the disease had entered its final phase. In the medieval mindset, as Sander Gilman has argued, the nose was an integral part of one's face and one's identity,[30] and indeed to be noseless left one "a non-person, no longer a full part of ... society."[31] Effectively socially dead, the lack of a nose was symbolic of a low social status. As justified by the book of Leviticus (21: 18), "the *denasti,* or noseless, were deemed ineligible for the priesthood because of their blemish, and presented ... a striking example of the connection between physical disfigurement and moral turpitude."[32]

The link between the noseless and those of low moral status can be seen throughout history. In medieval Venice female offenders had their noses cut off not only as punishment for a specific crime, but also as a future warning to others of their inherent unsociable behavior.[33] However, as early as Ancient Egyptian times, we find the association of *denasti* with sexual misconduct, where cutting off the nose was a punishment for adultery.[34] The *Ecloga*, the Byzantine legal code published in 726, continues this theme with laws 23 and 24 stating that carnal knowledge of a nun or virgin woman would result in a man having his nose slit.[35] Destruction of the nose was indicative of the destruction of one's honor, and specifically symbolized the incompleteness of one's body. Nowhere was this more clear than in the desperate acts of self-mutilation by nuns to stop invading forces raping them; both the nuns of St Cyr Monastery, Marseilles, under their abbess Eusebia, and those of Coldingham Priory in Scotland with their abbess Ebbe, carried out this extreme act to stop the Saracens and Vikings, respectively, from taking their virtue.[36] Elizabeth of Hungary similarly threatens such action when urged to remarry by her uncle after the death of her first husband.[37]

While, in the case of women, the loss of the nose is equated with the loss of sexual desirability, the loss of a nose for men had a different connotation.[38] As Aretaios noted, noselessness was equated with enhanced or immoral sexual desire; Frederick II (1194–1250) used this rationale in his punishment of those guilty of adultery, and males guilty of having favored prostitution, which involved the forced removal of the nose.[39]

Nearly all medieval depictions of lepers in literature are male. We have mentioned references to lepers in Troilus and Cressida, Tristan and Isolde, and Chaucer's Summoner, but visual depictions of lepers in manuscripts and bibles also tended to be male, as an internet image search using the term "medieval leper" can demonstrate.[40] Males then were the main targets of suspicion, and men were considered virulent and sexually dangerous. Robert Moore describes the male medieval lepers as being "endowed with an inordinate sexual appetites … incestuous … rapists … [who] sought to spread their condition by forced sexual intercourse with healthy persons."[41] Therefore, leprosy and lechery become interchangeable terms, as emphasized by Richard Rolle of Hampole's fourteenth-century *The Pricke of Conscience* stating: "And som, for ƺe syn of lechery, / Sal haf als ƺe yvel of meselry."[42] Further, the prominent mystic Margery Kempe also prayed for her son to be punished by God for his dissolute lifestyle and that his "synne of letchery [was] sone aftyr [punished], his face wex ful of whelys and bloberys *as it has ben a lepyr*."[43] And returning to the Summoner, Chaucer describes him "as hot … and lecherous" with a demeanor that frightened children.[44] Even the royal edicts mentioned earlier emphasized that lepers were perceived to be lecherous males of low social status, notably frequenters of brothels.

The threat of the lecherous leper was contained within their desire and potential to infect victims via carnal intercourse, insidiously contaminating the healthy. Susan Sontag notes that "leprosy in its heyday aroused a … disproportionate sense of horror [being] one of the most meaning-laden diseases, with victims being subject to outside projections of immorality, where feelings of evil are projected onto a disease and becoming increasingly meaning-laden, a hyperbole of the disease is projected back onto society."[45] As such, medieval leprosy became a socially constructed metaphor of moral and literal contagion, a symbol of the disgust associated with decay, pollution, anomie, weakness, and ugliness.[46] The leper becomes a social text, corruption made visible through a male emblem of decay,[47] enforcing the church teaching that sin was often the cause of bodily disease. Banished from the community the leper was a social outcast and considered loathsome; they were according to the Abbot of St Julian's hospital in St Albans, "to bear themselves as more to be despised and as more humble than all other men."[48] However, being humble was not necessarily a bad thing, for Jesus sided with the humble, and thus we move into exploring how the despised leper could, in certain circumstances, shift their social status. This rests on the notion of liminality and medieval theology, for while the leper was in everyday society an abhorrent outcast, a socially dead unwanted wanderer wearing his depravity, once contained within the liminal space of the leper hospital, his socially dead status and living dead appearance could be utilized by the church for religious purposes. It is at this stage that we need to elucidate medieval concepts of death and the afterlife.

The "Ideal" Leper and the Notion of Redemption

The "ideal" leper was a man who, due to theological interpretations of the body as essentially the mirror of the soul, wore his own moral sin as a physical deformity. This notion was perhaps most clearly expressed in Chaucer, where the Summoner in the *Canterbury Tales* is described as quintessentially a "good felawe,"[49] that is, one who inhabits the taverns and brothels, and a companion of pimps and prostitutes. This quite open debauchee[50] is not only sexually immoral but his overtly licentious behavior is a vivid symptom of deeper corruption: his clerical sin in obtaining financial gain through the abuse of his ecclesiastical power. This sinful behavior correlates with his leprosy. The representation of wearing one's inner sin outwardly is also found in the romantic tale of *Amis and Amiloun* where Amiloun contracts leprosy for deliberately disobeying God:[51] the character becomes "as foul a leper as ever was born in this world!"[52] Frightening and repulsive in everyday society for the contagious nature of his bodily and moral corruption, Amiloun wandered for several years as a beggar, but if he had been contained within a leprosaria, his spiritual and physical contagion could be perceived as semi-holy with the man living out his purgatorial punishment on earth.

Although Catholicism at the time acknowledged four afterlife destinations—heaven, hell, purgatory, and limbo—most people went to purgatory. Formulated in the Second Council of Lyons (1274), "purgatory ... [was] a halfway stage between earth and heaven, where the sinful but repentant ...

could, through purgatorial cleansing punishment, complete the process of making satisfaction for sin and so be rendered fit for heaven."[53] As expressed in Dante's *Comedy*, purgatorial punishment fitted one's earthly venial sins, so for example the greedy who enjoyed their material possessions shamelessly were bound and forced to lay on their stomachs and recite Psalm 119:25: *adhaesit pavimento anima mea* (my soul is attached onto dust), while the arrogant, being too erect in life, were made to carry rocks on their backs keeping their faces to the ground. One could lessen one's postmortem punishments through certain acts conducted in one's lifetimes, such as pilgrimage, praying for the dead, and purchasing indulgences. Further, in the wake of St Francis's (ca. 1181–1226) dramatic change in attitude toward lepers, shifting from repellence to active acceptance of, and servitude to, them, caring for lepers became another way of adding to one's Treasury of Merit: a Biblical inspired source of indulgence based on one doing good works that benefit others (Mt 6:19–20).

The role of the church in perceptions of leprosy is important here and helps explain the shift of lepers as social outcasts to effectively the elect of God. The Bible had always had an ambiguous relationship to leprosy, with the Torah/Old Testament seeing Aaron and Miriam temporarily punished with leprosy for the sin of speaking against Moses (Num 12:10–14), and the skin condition associated with uncleanliness and segregation (Lev 13:46, Num 5:2–4, 2 Kings 15:5, 2 Chron 26:16–21) as well as with the living dead, bodies half eaten away (Num 12:10–12, Job 18:13). However, in the New Testament, Jesus heals lepers (2 Kings 5:1–15, Mk 1:40–45, Lk 17:11–19) and his ability to heal leprosy is seen as a sign of his messiah-hood (Mt 11:5, Lk 7:22). Further, lepers were understood to have an elect status postmortem, which was evident in the Christian parable of the rich man and Lazarus the beggar (Lk 16:19–31). The Third Lateran Council (1179) noted that any disfiguring skin ailment was deemed leprous, and that lepers were "living dead ... barred from inheritance, denied the right to make gifts, unable to plead in court or negotiate contract."[54] Canon 23 then castigated lepers socially, even requiring them to wear identifying insignia, but although social outcasts they were given a status. The theological status of a leper dates to an edict from the Council of Lyon (583), which expressly forbade lepers to associate with the healthy. While this effectively placed them in the realms of the socially dead, it did mean that lepers needed to have their own churches and or cemeteries, with the benefit of a priest. Lepers might be marginalized and socially outcast from normative society, but the 583 edict ensured they were cared for spiritually, and the 1179 edict furthered this by requiring towns and cities with leper hospitals to house and feed lepers in their boundaries. Unable to work or care for themselves, these hospitals or *leprosaria*, provided shelter, food, and physical and spiritual care through the donations of alms, with the donors effectively buying some lessening of their purgatorial punishments through their charitable acts.

With a Christian theological imperative of acts of kindness toward to lepers, perhaps best exemplified through the Franciscan model of care for the leprous, together with perceived connections between the suffering Christ and the suffering leper,[55] it is perhaps unsurprising that from the twelfth to the fourteenth century we should find a number of saints engaging directly with lepers. Saint Thomas Beckett (d. 1170), Saint Hugh of Lincoln (d. 1200), Saint Elizabeth of Hungary (d. 1231), Saint Hedwig of Silisia (d. 1243), Saint Louis of France (d. 1270), and Saint Elzear of Sabran (d. 1323) are all notable for their pro-leper stances, licking lepers' sores, kissing leprous lips or feet, or noting the preferable status of living as a leper to dying of mortal sins.[56] Canon 22 of the Fourth Lateran Council (1215) correlates sickness of the body and the result of sin;[57] we thus find a number of contemporary sermons utilizing leprosy metaphorically to encourage proper Christian praxis. Jacques de Vitry (c. 1160–1240) discussed lepers as the elect of God in both his first and second sermon *ad lepros*: lepers will be certain of their celestial rewards, having endured suffering on earth rather than in purgatory, provided they devote their life to their spiritual health. Humbert of Romans (c. 1190–1277), in his composition of sermons for preachers, suggests those who visit lepers should be regarded as pious. He also noted that lepers should confess their sins and spend their days focusing on their afterlife, accepting with patience their current situation, "comforted by the example of Job."[58] Guilbert de Tournai (c. 1200–1284), another sermon writer, even went so far as to note that, as long as lepers resisted earthly temptations, after their death they would be nursed by Christ; the *leprosaria* was clearly the place they should be.[59]

The *Leprosaria* as Earthly Purgatory

The physically alive, but socially dead leprous individuals were forced to accept a new residence in the leprosaria.[60] Lepers were then liminal beings, bodies in transition, with individuals separated from their former lives but not yet integrated into a future state of being, residing in a liminal state of earthly purgatory before entering a final afterlife destination. The purgatorial status of the leper was further emphasized by their visibly fragmenting and rotting bodies. Caroline Walker Bynum posits that "because parts broke off the leper's body, because it fragmented and putrefied and became insensate when alive, in other words because it was a living death … it was used as a common metaphor for sin."[61] "Continuity of matter was necessary for continuity of the person,"[62] and bodily fragments were perceived to contain remnants of *spiritus*, which in turn contained inherent contagion. Thus, the decaying body of a leper represented the decaying social fabric and the manner in which sin could quite literally rot the soul. The medieval leprous body was a metaphor of social disorder, born of lechery, specifically related to the male, and disintegrating: it needed removal. The physical body was the body politic and the religious body, all in one.

Rawcliffe asserts that "the spots and stains of leprosy ... served as an effective metaphor for various manifestations of sin."[63] The assumption that spiritual deformity would somehow leave its trace upon the body as well as soul insidiously found its way into religious and secular literature alike. Not only physical, but also spiritual leprosy became threatening, as an anonymous fourteenth-century sermon states. For just as leprosy makes the body ugly and loathsome and repulsive, so the filth of lechery makes the soul spiritually very foul.[64] However, by entering purgatory prematurely, lepers had an unprecedented opportunity to pay off their purgatorial debt in this life rather than the next. As Bernard de Clairvaux (d. 1175) claimed, chronic disease was "a divine gift, pregnant with opportunity."[65] Anselm, too, proposed that "the progress of the soul grows out of the failure of the flesh, the salvation of the soul out of the illness of the flesh and forgiveness out of punishment."[66] Leprosy allowed the isolated victim to repent and atone for their sins, acting as a "spur to salvation."[67] Thus, "the leper had been granted the special grace of entering upon payment for his sins in this life, and could therefore look forward to earlier redemption in the next."[68] The leper in this sense was like the biblical figure of Job: he was especially beloved of God, and would win his reward in heaven for his sufferings on earth.[69] Considering the horrors that awaited in purgatorial afterlife, purgation before death seems to identify lepers as privileged, marked out by divine favor to suffer in this life, to lessen their suffering in the next.[70] However, lepers still occupied an unstable position within everyday society: lepers were socially undesirable, yet social examples, maintaining humility while experiencing a holy disease that would relieve their suffering in the afterlife.

To conclude, we have argued that medieval leprosy was a slowly progressive disease that contemporarily—in vernacular literature and theology—had close links to lechery and male sexuality. The obvious fragmentation of the body enabled accusation and ostracization, with formal diagnosis and moral censure of lepers being provided by the church. The loss of the nose in particular indicated the close relationship between sexual miscreancy and leprosy; however, royal edicts also associated this misbehavior with vagrants, vagabonds, and more generally the lower classes. Thus, a distinct image of the ideal leper is constructed: the nobility did not possess the qualities that pre-disposed them to leprosy, whereas the lewd, male, destitute poor were more liable to become infected. Leprosy was therefore intrinsically linked to gender and social status in medieval society. Lepers as liminal beings, betwixt and between states, required separation and segregation from their former communities. Their dissolving flesh being representative of postmortem decay, in turn indicated the leper's status as a purgatorial sufferer who needed to be contained and isolated within the walls of the leprosaria. With leprosy, the physical manifestation of the sins of the soul pedagogically informed those who witnessed the physical signs and symptoms of the disease: that immoral behavior will be punished either in this life, or more severely in purgatory. Therefore, as Bernard of Clairvaux, and Anselm proposed, leprosy as a physical disease of the soul was pregnant with opportunity. Lepers, as spiritual sufferers, could achieve early release from the torment of purgatory. But, as Rawcliffe posits, "embodying in his or her person a stark reminder of the ordeal to come, the leper cut a profoundly disturbing figure,"[71] and thus we suggest, the "ideal" male leper could be especially beloved by God, both holy and horrific.

Christina Welch is Senior Lecturer in Religious Studies at the University of Winchester.

Rohan Brown is Associate Lecturer in Religious Studies at the University of Winchester.

Notes

1. Carole Rawcliffe, *Leprosy in Medieval England* (Woodbridge: Boydell Press, 2006), 17.
2. Rawcliffe, *Leprosy,* 275.
3. Max Weber, *The Methodology of the Social Sciences* (Glencoe, IL: Free Press, 1924; reprinted 1949), 90.
4. Pierre J. G. Cabanis, *An Essay on the Certainty of Medicine,* trans. R. La Roche (Philadelphia: Robert Desilver, 1828), 104.
5. World Health Organization, "Transmission of Leprosy," accessed 24 August 2015, http://www.who.int/lep/transmission/en/
6. F. Lee and J. Magilton, "The Cemetery of the Hospital of St James and St Mary Magdalene Chichester—A Case Study," *World Archaeology* 21, no. 2 (1989): 278–279; Simon Roffey and Phil Marter, "St Mary Magdalene Hospital, Winchester," *Archaeology,* 17 (2011), accessed 24 August 2015, http://www.archaeologyuk.org/ba/ba117/feat2.shtml; Michael Farley and Keith Manchester, "The Cemetery of the Leper Hospital of St Margaret, High Wycombe, Buckinghamshire," *Medieval Archaeology* 33 (1989): 82–89.
7. Ian Mortimer, *The Time Traveller's Guide to Medieval England: A Handbook for Visitors to the Fourteenth Century* (New York: Vintage Books, 2009), 204.
8. Ibid., 204.
9. Michael Delahoyde, "The Summoner's Tale," accessed 24 August 2015, http://public.wsu.edu/~delahoyd/chaucer/SumT.html
10. Walter C. Curry, *Chaucer and the Medieval Sciences* (New York: Barnes and Noble, 1960), 395.
11. Caroline D. Eckhardt, *Chaucer's General Prologue to the Canterbury Tales: An Annotated Bibliography, 1900 to 1982* (Toronto: University of Toronto Press, 1990), 398.
12. Bryon Lee Grigsby, *Pestilence in Medieval and Early Modern English Literature* (London: Routledge, 2004), 84.

13. Michael Foucault, *The Archaeology of Knowledge* (London: Tavistock Publications, 1972), 16.
14. Saul Nathaniel Brody, *Disease of the Soul: Leprosy in Mediaeval Literature* (Ithaca: Cornell University Press, 1974), 103.
15. Bryan S. Turner, *The Body and Society: Explorations in Social Theory* (Oxford: Blackwell, 1984), 66–151.
16. Mary Douglas, "Witchcraft and Leprosy: Two Strategies of Exclusion," *Man, New Series* 26, no. 2 (1991): 732.
17. Johan Goudsblom, "Public Health and the Civilising Process," *Millbank Quarterly* 64, no. 2 (1986): 166.
18. Jeremy Seabrook, *Pauperland: Poverty and the Poor in Britain* (New York: Hurst Publishers, 2013), 21.
19. Ibid., 26.
20. Judy Ann Ford, *John Mirk's Festial: Orthodoxy, Lollardy and the Common People in Fourteenth-Century England* (Cambridge, D.S. Brewer, 2006): 71.
21. Ibid., 190.
22. Ibid., 275.
23. David Marcombe, *Leper Knights: The Order of St. Lazarus of Jerusalem in England, C.1150–1544* (Woodbridge: Boydell Press, 2004), 140
24. Jeffrey Richards, *Sex, Dissidence and Damnation* (London: Routledge, 1994), 160.
25. Samuel Lane, "A Course of Lectures on Syphilis: Lecture II," *The Lancet MDCCCXLI–XLII, in Two Volumes, Volume the First,* ed. Thomas Wakley, (London: George Churchill, 1841–1842): 281–286.
26. Franjo Gruber, Jasna Lipozenčić, and Tatjana Kehler, "History of Venereal Disease from Antiquity to Renaissance," *Acta Dermatovenerol Croat* 23, no. 1 (2015): 1–11.
27. Timothy S. Miller and John W. Nesbitt, *Walking Corpses: Leprosy in Byzantium and the Medieval West* (Ithaca: Cornell University Press, 2014), 157.
28. Richards, *Sex, Dissidence and Damnation,* 160.
29. Rawcliffe, *Leprosy,* 140.
30. Sander Gilman, *Making the Body Beautiful: A Cultural History of Aesthetic Surgery* (Princeton, NJ: Princeton University Press, 1999), xx.
31. Patricia Skinner, "The Gendered Nose and Its Lack: 'Medieval' Nose-Cutting and Its Modern Manifestations," *Journal of Women's History* 26, no. 1 (2014): 50.
32. Valentin Groebner, "Losing Face, Saving Face: Noses and Honour in the Late Medieval Town," *History Workshop Journal* 60 (1995): 1–15.
33. Nella Lonza, "On Cutting off Noses and Pulling out Beards: Face as a Medium of Crime and Punishment in Medieval Dubrovnik," in *Our Daily Crime,* ed. Gordon Ravančić (Zagreb: Hrvatski Institut za Povijest, 2014), 61.
34. G. Sperati, "Amputation of the Nose Throughout History," *Acta Otorhinolaryngol Italy* 29, no. 1 (2009): 44–50.
35. Martha A. Brozyna, ed., *Gender and Sexuality in the Middle Ages: A Medieval Source Documents Reader* (Jefferson: McFarland and Co., 2005), 110.
36. For nuns of St Cyr, see Liz Wilson, *Charming Cadavers: Horrific Figurations of the Feminine in Indian Buddhist Hagiographic Literature* (Chicago: University of Chicago Press, 1996), 172; for nuns of Coldingham, see Rev. J. B. Mackinlay, *St. Edmund, King and Martyr* (New York: London and Leamington Art and Book Company, 1893), 109.
37. See Larissa Traacy, *Women of the Gilte Legende: A Selection of Middle English Saints' Lives* (Cambridge: D.S. Brewer, 2003), 63.

38. Corinne J. Saunders, *Rape and Ravishment in the Literature of Medieval England* (Cambridge: D.S. Brewer, 2001), 141, 145.
39. Giorgio Sperati, "Amputation of the Nose throughout History," *Acta Otorhinolaryngol Ital* 29, no. 1 (2009): 44–50, accessed 24 August 2015, http://www.ncbi.nlm.nih.gov/pmc/articles/PMC2689568/.
40. See, for example, accessed 24 August 2015, https://web.stanford.edu/class/humbio103/ParaSites2006/Leprosy/Historical_files/image008.jpg.
41. Robert Ian Moore, *The Formation of a Persecuting Society* (Oxford: Oxford University Press, 1987), 54–55.
42. Richard Rolle of Hampole, *The Pricke of Conscience: Stimulus Conscientiae: A Northumbrian Poem,* ed. Richard Morris (London: A. Asher, 1863), 82.
43. Margery Kempe, *The Book of Margery Kempe: Vol. 1,* ed. Sanford Brown Meech (London: Oxford University Press, 1940), 221–223.
44. Chaucer cited in Moore, *Formation of a Persecuting Society,* 54–55.
45. Susan Sontag cited in Marcia Gaudet, "Telling It Slant: Personal Narrative, Tall Tales, and the Reality of Leprosy," *Western Folklore* 49, no. 2 (1990): 193.
46. Goudsblom, "Public Health," 194.
47. Ibid.
48. John Stuart, "Archaeological Essays by the late Sir James T. Simpson, Baet, Vol. II," accessed 1 September 2014, http://archive.org/stream/archaeologicales02simpuoft/archaeologicales02simpuoft_djvu.txt, 136 and William Page, "Hospital of St Julian by St Albans," in *A History of the County of Hertfordshore, Vol. IV,* ed. William Page, accessed 1 September 2014, http://www.british-history.ac.uk/report.aspx?compid=37985, 464–467.
49. Geoffrey Chaucer, "The Summoner," *The Canterbury Tales,* accessed 24 August 2015, http://www.librarius.com/canttran/genpro/genpro625-670.htm.
50. Richard Firth Green, "The Sexual Normality of Chaucer's Pardoner," accessed 24 August 2015, http://sites.fas.harvard.edu/~chaucer/canttales/pardt/pard-gre.htm.
51. See lines 1250–1270 in Ken Eckert, "Chaucer's Reading List: Sir Thopas, Auchinleck, and Middle English Romances in Translation," (PhD diss., University of Nevada, 2011), accessed 1 September 2014, http://digitalscholarship.unlv.edu/cgi/viewcontent.cgi?article=2037&context=thesesdissertations, 50.
52. *Amis and Amiloun,* trans. Edith Ricket (Cambridge: Middle English Series, 2000), 17.
53. Rosemary Horrox, "Purgatory, Prayer and Plague: 1150–1380," in *Death in England: An Illustrated History,* ed. Peter Jupp and Clare Gittings (Manchester: Manchester University Press, 2000), 90.
54. Elaine Clark, "Social Welfare and Mutual Aid in the Medieval Countryside," *Journal of British Studies* 33, no.4 (1994): 396.
55. *Holkham Bible,* Add MS 47683, accessed 24 August 2015, http://www.bl.uk/manuscripts/FullDisplay.aspx?ref=Add_MS_47682; Carol Rawcliffe, "The Lost Hospitals of London: Leprosaria" (lecture delivered at Gresham College, London, 3 May 2012), accessed 24 August 2015, http://www.gresham.ac.uk/lectures-and-events/the-lost-hospitals-of-london-leprosaria.
56. Kay Brainerd Slocumb, *Liturgies in Honour of Thomas Becket* (Toronto: University of Toronto Press, 2004), 89; Decima L. Douie and D. Hugh Farmer, eds. *Magna Vitae Sancti Hugonis: The Life of St. Hugh of Lincoln* (Oxford: Clarendon Press, 1985), 2:84; Kenneth Baxter World, *The Life and Afterlife of St. Elizabeth*

of Hungary (Oxford: Oxford University Press, 2010), 69; Gábor Klaniczay, *Holy Rulers and Blessed Princesses: Dynastic Cults in Medieval Central Europe* (Cambridge: Cambridge University Press, 2002), 203; Joseph Vann, "Saint Louis—Confessor, King Of France—1214–1270 Feast: August 25," accessed 1 September 2014, http://www.ewtn.com/library/mary/louis.htm; and Christine M. Boeckl, *Images of Leprosy: Disease, Religion and Politics in European Art* (Kirksville, MO: Truman State University Press, 2011), 88.

57. Irina Metzler, *Disability in Medieval Europe: Thinking about Physical Impairment during the High Middle Ages, c. 1100–1400* (London: Routledge, 2006), 47.
58. Humbert of Romans cited in Courtney A. Krolikoski, "Malady or Miracle? The Influence of St Frances on the Perception of Leprosy in the High Middle Ages" (MA thesis, Central European University, 2011), 140.
59. Ibid.
60. Clark, "Social Welfare," 40.
61. Caroline Walker Bynum, *Fragmentation and Redemption* (New York: Zone Books, 1992), 276.
62. Caroline Walker Bynum, "Material Continuity, Personal Survival, and the Resurrection of the Body: A Scholastic Discussion in Its Medieval and Modern Contexts," *History of Religions* 30, no. 1 (1990): 81.
63. Rawcliffe, *Leprosy*, 48.
64. Anon in John Small, ed., *English Metrical Homilees* (Edinburgh, 1862), 129–130.
65. De Clairvaux cited in Rawcliffe, *Leprosy*, 56.
66. Anselm of Canterbury, *The Letters of St. Anselm of Canterbury, Vol. 1.* (Ann Arbor: University of Michigan Press, 1990), 163.
67. Rawcliffe, *Leprosy*, 53.
68. Martyn Whittock, *A Brief History of Life in the Middle Ages: Scenes from the Town and Countryside of Medieval England* (London: Robinson, 2009), 209.
69. Rawcliffe, *Leprosy*, 57.
70. Ibid., 59.
71. Ibid., 137.

Chapter 5

"To take a wyf"
Marriage, Status, and Moral Conduct in "The Merchant's Tale"

Natalie Hanna

Chaucer's "The Merchant's Tale" approaches the subjects of marriage, status, and moral conduct in the style of fabliau, using humor and satire to consider some more tangible fears of the medieval period.[1] Such concerns within marriage include power and dominance, age and adultery; all of which are explored in the narrative through a combination of the more elevated language of courtly romance and that of the "low-footed" fabliau.[2] Due to this amalgamation of genres, the text is comprised of a particularly wide range of gender-based noun terms related to marriage, class, and conduct (for example, "cokewold," "housbonde," "knight," "lady," "shrewe," "wyf") to define the characters and their actions. While much scholarship has been carried out regarding gender and power dynamics in the text, as well as the moral implications of the tale within a medieval social context, such gendered language has not been considered.[3] However, there has been some critique on aspects of status, predominantly concerning age within medieval marriage. Margaret Hallissy's article "Widow-To-Be: May in Chaucer's 'The Merchant's Tale'" and Stephen J. Russell's examination on "Chaucer's Old Men" explore the social implications for a young May marrying aged Januarie in light of social practices of the medieval period, each focusing on female and male roles respectively.[4] However, no study has taken a linguistic approach when examining the narrative's treatment of gender, nor has one considered a comparative study of gender terminology in the text. This article uses a corpus of *The Canterbury Tales* to examine the gender terms in "The Merchant's Tale" to demonstrate how social concerns surrounding marital status are revealed through these words and their phraseology.

Marital Terms in "The Merchant's Tale"

Marriage and status is a central theme to the tale, made apparent from the opening, which dedicates the first 463 lines to Januarie's deliberation and justification of marrying in his old age, and the picking of his ideal wife. In his lengthy debate on the virtues and vices of wives and marriage, the word "wyf" is the most frequently occurring of these gender terms in the tale. While discussion of a wife's role is fundamental to this narrative, the occurrence of "wyf" is nonetheless notably extensive, appearing 61 times throughout the tale, its prologue and its epilogue. This equates to 18 percent of the word's overall use in *The Canterbury Tales* corpus, and is the highest use of the term in any one of the *Tales*. Moreover, when compared to other narratives of similar lengths in which the term also frequently occurs, such as "The Wife of Bath's Prologue and Tale" and "The Clerk's Tale," "The Merchant's Tale" is found to contain a much greater use of "wyf," as shown in Table 5.1:[5]

Table 5.1 The most frequent use of "wyf" in *The Canterbury Tales* corpus.

Text	Number of Occurrences	Overall Use in Canterbury Tales	Line Length of Text
Merchant's Tale	61	18%	1227
Wife of Bath's Tale	43	13%	1264
Clerk's Tale	38	11%	1220
Parson's Tale	27	8%	1080
Shipman's Tale	24	7%	452

The use of the term in "The Merchant's Tale" is, thus, linguistically significant. "Wyf" is also distinctive when compared to other words used to denote gender roles in the tale, the occurrence of which are presented in Table 5.2:

Table 5.2 The total use of selected gender-based noun terms in "The Merchant's Tale."

Noun Term	Number of Occurrences
Wyf	61
Sire	11
Knyght	9
Lady	8
Lord	7
Squier	5
Housbonde	4
Shrewe	3
Cokewold	2
Wenche	1

"Wyf" occurs far more frequently than any other term, shown here as appearing 50 times more than the second most frequently occurring term, "sire." With this in mind, the language of "The Merchant's Tale" appears to be most concerned with the role of a "wyf" in *The Canterbury Tales*. Yet, upon further consideration of the text's language and phrasing it seems that it is not only the position of "wyf" that is under scrutiny, but also that of the correlative role of "housbonde" and, in particular, Januarie's inability to fulfill what is expected of this status. This is notable through the lack of use of the word itself, occurring only four times, as well as the lack of discussion of a husband's role in the marriage in comparison to the extensive discussion of a wife's. This study will, therefore, comparatively examine the presentation of gender and marriage through analysis of the language used to denote Januarie and May's marital statuses, focusing firstly on the discussion of "wyf" and secondly of that of "housbonde."

Wyf

Throughout the opening lines of the tale, "wyf" is used repeatedly as ageing Januarie considers the use of a wife and the worth of marriage. It is perhaps not surprising, in light of critical work on gender and status in the tale, such as that of Hallissy and Kim Phillips, that the language surrounding the term indicates a medieval woman's economic, social, and moral value granted through marriage.[6] This is revealed through the semantic field of the noun terms around "wyf," which contain connotations of personal property, economic worth, and servitude. Words such as "tresor," "londes," "rentes," "pasture," "commune," and "yifte," which fall under a semantic category of property and income, are found in close proximity to "wyf." Januarie insists that just as these possessions are gifts of fortune, a wife is God's gift to man, suggesting a man's unquestionable right to a wife that has been conferred by divine authority.[7] In the second half of his speech he considers the age and physical attributes of his ideal spouse, using language that falls primarily into the semantic field of food, including "fish," "pyk," "boef," "veel," and "bene-straw" (beanstalk).[8] The comparison of a wife to food reflects not only Januarie's preoccupation with a wife's market-worth, but also his desire for her as one who can satisfy his sexual appetite. This is an image made more explicit when, following the consummation of his marriage, Januarie's first action is to eat bread in bed, gratifying his sexual desire and physical hunger simultaneously. Further language surrounding the term can be seen to support Januarie's belief in ownership of his wife and his desire that her primary role in marriage will be to serve him. This includes adjectives and verbs depicting his ideal wife's actions: "trewe," "ententyf," "serve," "helpe," "obeye," and "humble," each connoting a serving role.[9] In addition to such concerns of her economic worth, another of Januarie's ideal traits is that of his future wife's youth, explaining the merits of marrying a "yong thyng" that can be easily molded, likening such a woman to warm candle wax.[10] Her youth is of utmost importance to Januarie who, despite being "passed sixty yeer," is explicit that he will not marry a woman older than twenty years, stating twice that he will "noon oold wyf han."[11] Januarie's outlandish belief that a woman half his age is too old for him is comical, yet, although exaggerated, it reflects an increasingly common viewpoint in medieval society. Phillips explains in her examination of young women in medieval England why Januarie's beliefs were not altogether surprising for the period, that although he "was being satirized as an old man with unsuitable desires … his ideal was a common one … Increasingly, youth was becoming a necessary element of ideal femininity."[12] Youth was seen to indicate a woman's beauty and fertility, but these are not the only qualities that make marrying a young bride preferable for Januarie. He seems to be most motivated by the fact that he does not want to marry a widow. "Wydwes," he explains, are too knowledgeable of marital relationships and thus are inclined to deceive men.[13] His fear of marrying such a woman alludes to the widow's greater social and, often, financial power than a "mayde" or "wyf" in medieval society. Hallissy describes the freedom that the status of "wydwe" granted a woman, as "widowhood conferred *sui juris* status, which constituted a woman's first independence."[14] She continues that the "wide age discrepancy between the marriage partners" that was favored for widowers or men who married later in life in the Middle Ages meant that the young women frequently outlived their husbands, or perhaps several husbands, and thus, "the widow's economic sufficiency gave her heightened power in the marriage market, which in turn could enable her to increase her wealth even further. Undoubtedly some men, like Januarie, disliked widows for their knowledge and assertiveness."[15] Januarie is interested only in marrying a woman he can control, "gye" and dominate, so a widow with greater social rights or financial independence is not desirable.[16] It is for this reason that he must marry someone so young: one he can be certain has not gained any such economic position or knowledge. Though satirized, his standards allow the text to explore the fear of some men of the period of marrying women who carried the status of "wydwe" and the ulterior motives one may have for marrying a "yong thyng," aside from her ability to reproduce. The irony, of course, is revealed when Januarie's carefully selected young bride proves as deceiving as he fears an older widow would be.

As shown, Januarie's frequent use of "wyf" reflects his preoccupation with how the qualities of a spouse will benefit him as "the fruyt of his tresor," referring to her economic, social, and moral value.[17] Yet what appears most notable concerning his speech is that of the 40 instances when he utters the word, only six are in reference to his actual wife, May. The remaining 36 uses refer to hypothetical descriptions, generalizations, and idealizations he envisions for his future wife. Chaucer's application of the term in this way emphasizes Januarie's obsession with his ideal image of marriage, rather than the reality of it. His metaphorical blindness, heightened by his physical blindness later in the tale, concerns not only May's deception and adultery, but can be extended to his entire approach to marriage. This is demonstrated particularly through his flawed references to wives from classical and biblical sources. Peggy Knapp noted of Janaurie's examples of wives as justification of his desire to marry that, "he choose[s] four Old Testament women whose resourceful actions did not necessarily benefit their husbands."[18] This, together with his flawed understanding of classical philosophers' discussions on marriage, such as that of the Aristotelian Theophrastus, portrays the extent of Januarie's figurative blindness, manipulating contrasting advice to support his own argument. When Januarie does eventually call May his "wyf" it correlates with the loss of control he feels in the relationship. This takes place around two-thirds into the tale, when having gone blind, Januarie decides he wants to "pleye" in the garden.[19] He addresses May as follows:

> Rys up, my wyf, my love, my lady free!
> . . .
> The gardyn is enclosed al aboute;
> Com forth, my white spouse! Out of doute
> Thou hast me wounded in myn herte, O wyf!
> . . .
> I chees thee for my wyf and my confort.[20]

Here Januarie orders May out to the garden he has created especially to confine her in, allowing them to engage in sexual activity undisturbed, as well as enabling him to ensure her fidelity as he alone has access to the space. Thus, when he finally uses the term "wyf" to directly refer to her, and does so repeatedly, it is to remind her of her role and duty to serve him as his spouse. However, now that Januarie is blind he is also at his weakest point physically in the text, and the narrator notes the "outrageous" jealousy he feels having lost his ability to keep a close eye on her.[21] His jealousy grows to the point that he will not allow May to go anywhere unless "he had hond on hire alway," allowing him to dictate her movements even without his sight, and as he continues to grow more insecure it is not long until he begins to call her "wyf."[22] The repeated use of the address is another means by which he can exercise his control over her, reminding her of her relational duties to him and her marital debt. The irony of this scene is made strikingly apparent when, ordering her into the enclosed space to limit her movements, he calls her his "lady free."[23] Januarie continues his speech, referring to her three more times as "wyf" as he explains her position and tells her to submit to his sexual desires. Having told her to "Rys up" and "Com forth" he now explains to her why she should be true to him, addressing her with "Now wyf" and "trewe deere wyf."[24] He says she should be true for the love of Christ, her own honor and the wealth and land she shall inherit from him before instructing her, "Now kys me, wyf, and lat us rome aboute."[25] The term "wyf" is a means for Januarie to instruct May to do as he wishes: to go the garden, to fulfill his sexual desires, and to justify why she should remain true to him even though he is blind. Therefore, Janaurie first calls May "wyf" and continues to do so only in this scene because the term itself is a means of asserting dominance over his young spouse in his weakened and frail state. However, this is also the first time that Januarie actually perceives May as his wife; the fact that it takes physical blindness to see her this way only heightens the sense of the metaphorical blindness he has suffered until this point. Although Januarie is speaking the term and noting May's status as his wife for the first time, her actions, however, are simultaneously resisting the role he is enforcing upon her. During this same exchange, May signs to Damien to enter the garden and to climb the pear tree, directly opposing Januarie's attempts of control, and creating the final, fabliau-esque scene. Januarie's exasperated use of "wyf" highlights May's resistance to the role and, as he tries to assert his dominance through his language, she comes closer to defying him.

While the language discussed thus far—denoting youth, market-worth, and servitude—is not altogether unexpected to associate with the status of a medieval wife, the most commonly collocating phrase is more surprising. "Take a wyf" is repeated on seven occasions, twice with the addition of the adjective "yong" and three times the phrase is preceded by "to":

> "To take a wyf it is a glorious thyng"
> "Thanne sholde he take a yong wyf and a feir"
> "And if thou take a wyf unto thyn hoold"
> "For whiche causes man sholde take a wyf."
> "To take a yong wyf; by my fader kyn"
> "Take hym a wyf with greet devocioun"
> "To take a wyf withouten avysement."[26]

Januarie is the only person to utter these phrases, and he does so during his opening consideration of marriage. From analysis of the entire corpus of *The Canterbury Tales*, the phrase "take a" is found to be solely associated with the gender term "wyf," only occurring in direct reference to this female marital status. One instance is found in "The Clerk's Tale," along with another similar phrase "take another wyf," which will be discussed in the next section of this analysis. However, as shown, "take a wyf" appears almost exclusively in "The Merchant's Tale" and, as Januarie is the sole character to utter it, the idea of "taking" a wife is associated specifically with his attitude to wives and conduct in marriage. The phrase structure syntactically deems "a wyf" the object of the utterance, reiterating Januarie's objectification of a wife as his property once he has married her. Moreover, in Middle English the term "take" connotes particularly negative actions that provide further understanding of Januarie's self-satisfying intentions for marriage. In the medieval period especially, "take" evokes associations with capture, greed, and selfishness, and it connotes specific actions to women including, to "bring (a woman) forcibly into one's household."[27] Although the verb can also connote more positive senses with regards to "taking" a person, such as "to receive into one's company, care" that one could propose as Januarie's intentions to take a wife, the term was far more commonly associated with a sense of wrong doing.[28] This idea of wrongfully seizing a wife is further stressed through the inclusion of the characters Pluto and Proserpina in later scenes of the tale. Pluto and Proserpina's presence in the text acts as a "mirror image" of Januarie and May's relationship, as Elizabeth Simmons-O'Neill describes in her article on the associations drawn between Pluto and Januarie: "both Pluto and Januarie are feckless old men whose wives, taken initially against their own will and Nature's, have accepted their lot and learned to keep the upper hand in marriage."[29] Pluto's capture and rape of Proserpina draws a clear connection between this couple and Janaurie's plans to "take a wyf," reinforcing negative connotations of the phrase and its reference to Janaurie's desires to marry.

Housbonde

The text's concern with taking a wife becomes more apparent in light of an examination of the corresponding marital status of "housbonde" in the text. As shown in Table 5.2, there is scarcely any mention of "housbonde"; the term is used only four times compared to the 61 uses of "wyf." This lack of use is unexpected, if it is compared with Chaucer's texts that also include a high frequency of the term "wyf." For example, as shown in Table 5.1, "The Wife of Bath's Prologue and Tale" contain the second highest use of "wyf" in *The Canterbury Tales*, appearing 43 times. Yet here the term "housbonde" is also found at a high frequency of 25 occurrences. This balance is reiterated throughout all other narratives within *The Canterbury Tales* that mention "wyf" and "housbonde," making the disparity in "The Merchant's Tale" all the more significant. In this tale the word is used by the narrator only when describing hypothetical images of husbands that Januarie thinks upon during his deliberation of marriage, and once in reference to the Old Testament's Nabal during Januarie's misjudged discussion of obedient wives.[30] Januarie's reference to Nabal again demonstrates his ignorance, making reference to a marriage where the wife's ingenuity results in her husband's demise.[31] These descriptions all take place at the beginning of the tale during the narrator's report on what Januarie thinks marriage will entail, but the term is never used to actually reference Januarie, even after he has legally become a husband. The fact that "housbonde" is used at all in the text, however, is crucial to the presentation of the old knight. This is because it demonstrates that the word exists in the vocabulary of the text and is available for use by the characters, but Chaucer has purposefully chosen to omit using it in descriptions of Januarie. Instead, another, more frequently occurring phrase with similar connotations, "wedded man," is found in place of "housbonde" when describing his marital status. This phrase and its plural and possessive variations, "wedded men" and "wedded mannes," are found on nine occasions in "The Merchant's Tale," which, although a small number, is significant as these phrases only appear 13 times in the whole *Canterbury Tales* corpus.[32] The phrase appears in "The Shipman's Tale," "The Clerk's Tale," and "The Merchant's Tale," and far more frequently in the latter, rendering it particularly significant to this text's presentation of the male marital role. While aspects of style, rhyme, and meter might explain this alternative identification of Januarie's status, there also appears to be a semantic reason for the labeling of the old knight as a "wedded man." The phrase is among the first descriptions that the reader receives of Januarie, distinguishing him in this role from the opening lines, as the narrator explains:

> Were it for hoolynesse or for dotage
> I kan nat seye, but swich a greet corage
> Hadde this knyght to been a wedded man
> That day and nyght he dooth al that he kan
> T'espien where he myghte wedded be.[33]

The narrator tells of Januarie's desire and motivation to marry, explaining that he wants to be "a wedded man," spending day and night trying to come up with a way to be "wedded." From this description, and Januarie's subsequent explanation of the sexual and moral gratification he may obtain through marriage, his motivations to marry do not appear to arise from courtly love or any other desire to serve a woman as her husband. His motives, therefore, are quite different from those of other characters in the *Canterbury Tales* who fight and suffer to win their wife's love, such as Palamon in "The Knight's Tale," who suffers years of lovesickness for Emily, and Arveragus in "The Franklin's Tale," who "loved and dide his payne" in pursuit of his wife's hand in marriage.[34] Although the narrator is reluctant to speculate over Januarie's true motives, stating he "kan nat seye," Januarie's domineering and sexual desires are foregrounded through the imagery and language in his debate, as demonstrated in his wish to take a young wife.[35] Semantically the term "housbonde" denotes not only a man in marriage, but specifically one "Correlative to *wife*."[36] The fact that the term is not used to denote Januarie, and the more semantically detached "a wedded man" is found in its place, reflects his belief that his wife should serve him with little concern for his role in the partnership. Januarie does not express any interest in being a "housbonde" but only to be wedded. Reinforcing this portrayal, all of the men in the text—Januarie (himself), Justinus, Placebo, and the Merchant narrator—recognize Januarie as a "wedded man" instead of a "housbonde." This usage hints toward Januarie's inability to fulfill what is expected of the role of a husband in medieval society. Januarie's age would lead the reader to question his abilities to reproduce, one which he is aware of himself as he insists on his abilities to do so to Justinus and Placebo when justifying his case for marriage.[37] Hallissy argues that, based on May's reaction to Januarie's sexual abilities, it is unlikely she would be able to conceive, because of the medieval correlation between "female pleasure and conception."[38] Thus, the lack of use of "housbonde" may reflect Januarie's inability to be granted the status because he cannot satisfy his wife, in addition to his lack of concern with the role itself. This connotation of the phrase can be supported by the one occurrence of the plural "wedded men" in "The Shipman's Tale." The monk John, when asked by the wife why he is out of bed so early in the morning, responds with:

> "Nece," quod he, "it oghte ynough suffise
> Fyve houres for to slepe upon a nyght,
> But it were for an old appalled wight,
> As been thise wedded men, that lye and dare."[39]

John describes wedded men as old feeble creatures that need to lie and doze, and directly associates this with sexual stamina when, a few lines later, he asks her if the reason she needs sleep is because she has been put to work since the night began, blushing at his improper thought. Through this statement John hints at the old husband's impotence, forcing his wife to "labor" throughout the night, and, thus, drawing a semantic connection between the wedded man and one who lacks the ability to fulfill a husband's sexual duty.

Further semantic associations with this phrase can be gathered from the three other uses found in the *Canterbury Tales* corpus, which help to clarify a reading of the language employed in "The Merchant's Tale." These are found in "The Clerk's Tale," first occurring at the beginning of the tale in reference to Walter, when his citizens urge him to marry so that he may produce an heir. They tell him, "We myghte lyven in moore felicitee … if it youre wille be, / That for to been a wedded man."[40] Here the wedded man refers to one who marries as more of an economic transaction than out of love, intending the union as a means of guaranteeing Walter's lineage. More explicitly negative connotations are felt in the final two instances of the phrase. "Wedded man" is used in the "Lenvoy de Chaucer" that follows "The Clerk's Tale," in which Chaucer makes a point of commenting on Walter's cruel treatment of his wife and her acceptance of his behavior, warning that no "wedded man" should test his wife as Walter did and expect her to show the same patience as Griselda:

> No wedded man so hardy be t'assaille
> His wyves pacience in trust to fynde
> Grisildis, for in certein he shal faille.[41]

Chaucer's reference to Walter and one who wants to test their wife as a "wedded man" associates the role with one who desires control over his spouse. The association with Walter particularly hints toward a "wedded man" as one who treats his wife in a cruel or objectionable manner because of this need to dominate and control. Walter's reasons for ruthlessly testing Griselda are not clear; the narrator makes numerous comments on how unnecessary his actions are, and by the final test in section four of the tale he notes how Walter could not stop regardless if his intentions were "for ernest ne for game."[42] The suggestion that Walter may be treating his wife so cruelly for his own pleasure further associates the "wedded man" with a particularly deplorable husband who desires his wife to serve him regardless of his treatment of her. This idea is outlined more explicitly in the third use of the phrase, with the plural variation "wedded men" appearing also in the fourth section of the tale. The narrator interjects here to explain Walter's continued testing of Griselda, stating that "But wedded men ne knowe no mesure, / Whan that they fynde a pacient creature."[43] "Wedded men" refers to those, then, who can show no self-restraint in dominating their wives when they find a patient woman like Griselda. These connotations are particularly significant to Januarie because, as a reader, we know that Chaucer intended "The Clerk's Tale" and "The Merchant's Tale" to be read in order, as the Merchant recounts his tale in response to the Clerk's, lamenting how there is a great difference between patient Griselda and his shrewish wife.[44] Therefore, the repeated use of "wedded man" to denote Walter and Januarie in *The Canterbury Tales* appears not as coincidence, but to encourage the reader to reflect on Januarie's behavior in light of Walter's. In his envoy, Chaucer clearly advises against Griselda's acceptance of the oppression that Walter places upon her, instructing women not to allow their husbands to exploit them because of their youth, stating "Beth nat bidaffed [outwitted] for youre innocence."[45] Januarie marries the youthful May so that he can control and manipulate her, recalling Walter's dominance of Griselda in the preceding tale. The status "wedded man" can be seen, therefore, to contain connotations of one who mistreats his wife, or displays excessive desire to control her, in addition to one who is detached from the partnership or unable to fulfill the role of "housbonde" in the marriage. The example provided by Walter and Griselda in the previous tale may allow for further understanding for May's resistance to Januarie's control, while also heightening the ironic tone of the narrative, as Januarie's attempts at dominance are in stark contrast to Walter's control of Griselda, because they result only in his cuckolding.

The association of the role of a "wedded man" and Januarie and Walter's treatment of their wives is further understood when reconsidering the use of the phrase "to take a wyf" discussed previously. As noted "take a wyf" appears almost exclusively in "The Merchant's Tale"; however, one instance of "taak a wyf" and a similar phrase "take another wyf" are found in "The Clerk's Tale." The former phrase appears at the opening of "The Clerk's Tale" when Walter's citizens ask him to "taak a wyf, for hye Goddes sake!" for fear that he will die without leaving them an heir.[46] Walter then later uses a related phrase himself when testing Griselda for the final time, telling her how he will remarry, saying his people have asked him "to take / Another wyf."[47] This connects Januarie and Walter's domineering approach to marriage and the phrase "take a wyf," furthering its negative connotations. In doing so it also associates the "wedded man" as the marital status of one who "takes" a wife, distinguishing such objectionable behavior from that of a "housbonde." Both men focus on how their wives should serve them and choose young women of lower social status, suggesting that their ability to give them rank fulfills their part in the marriage. Yet, through the disparity in their marital statuses the text criticizes these beliefs, showing that bestowing rank or financial status is not enough to qualify as a "housbonde." This evidence builds on work by Simmons-O'Neill, who shows how Chaucer's use of classical goddesses in *The Canterbury Tales* "suggests a continuing concern ... with the issue of how women are defined by more powerful men."[48] The language of "The Merchant's Tale" can certainly be seen to explore this issue through Januarie and Walter. Both are determined to have dominance over their spouses, and so are connected through the use of "take a wyf": a phrase used solely to connote their emotional and, in Januarie's case, physical inability to fulfill the role of "housbonde," and locating them in the semantically detached role of "wedded men."

Conclusion

A comparative analysis of marital statuses in "The Merchant's Tale" demonstrates expected associations of aspects of trade and economic value concerning wives. However, it also reveals a new idea in Chaucer's work of "taking" a wife through such trade, rather than a concept of mutual affection or courtly love. Status is revealed as both a means of control and resistance for Januarie and May, and the lack of unity in their marital partnership is expressed through the imbalanced use of "wyf" and "housbonde." The overuse of "wyf" in contrast to the complete lack of discussion of May herself ridicules the basing of a woman's actual role in marriage on idealistic exemplars of wives throughout literature and history. The study also reveals how Chaucer employs the status "wedded man" as a means of semantically distinguishing a "housbonde"—one in mutual correlation to his wife—from those who cannot fulfill the position and are not concerned with their role in the partnership. The association of Walter and Januarie's marital roles through this phrasing enables the text to raise concerns over those that present self-satisfying desires for marriage, as both men imply they are marrying to produce heirs but demonstrate more abusive motives for taking poor, young wives. Ultimately, the satirical tone throughout "The Merchant's Tale," and May's successful opposition to Januarie's control prevents both characters from transcending the fabliau stereotypes of adulteress wife and cuckolded husband, but nonetheless these profound social concerns of the age are raised through the terming of their marital statuses.

Natalie Hanna is Lecturer in English at the University of Liverpool.

Notes

1. Critics debate whether or not the genre of this tale is in keeping with the more comic of Chaucer's fabliaux, such as "The Miller's Tale" or "The Summoner's Tale," or if it encourages a moral reading alongside such comic elements, as seen with the style of "The Pardoner's Tale." Nevertheless, it may still be felt to contain strong elements of fabliaux even if a moral reading can also be deduced. For readings of the tale's "amorality," see Helen Cooper, *Oxford Guides to Chaucer* (Oxford: Oxford University Press, 1996), 96. For an interpretation of the text as a "moral fabliau," see J. A. Burrow, "Irony in the Merchant's Tale," *Anglia* 75, no. 2 (1957): 199–208.
2. Donatus calls fable "low-footed" because "of the lowness of its argument." This view is held by classical figures such as Aristotle, Cicero, and Donatus, who felt that the comic genre, which includes fabliau and fable, are of low intellect and a mark of the work of lower classes, as "comedy goes against the more intellectual goals of rhetoric." See Mary E. Leech, "That's Not Funny: Comic Forms, Didactic Purpose, and Physical Injury in Medieval Comic Tales," *LATCH: A Journal for the Study of the Literary Artifact in Theory, Culture, or History* 1 (2008): 105–127, at 109–110.
3. For example, see Huriye Reis, "Chaucer's Fabliau Women: Paradigms of Resistance and Pleasure," *Journal of Faculty of Letters* 29, no. 2 (2012): 123–135, and Alcuin Blamires, *Chaucer, Ethics and Gender* (Oxford: Oxford University Press, 2006), 78–105.
4. Margaret Hallissy, "Widow-To-Be: May in Chaucer's 'The Merchant's Tale,'" *Studies in Short Fiction* 26, no. 3 (1989): 295–304; Stephen J. Russell, "Chaucer's Old Men," *Medieval Perspectives* 23 (2008): 85–96.
5. The data from the *Tales* presented in Tables 5.1 and 5.2 includes any prologues or epilogues that accompany the texts. The occurrences recorded refer to the single case of the noun term only, and includes any variations of spelling. For

further discussion of the statistical frequency of 'wyf' in "The Merchant's Tale" and across the *Canterbury Tales* in relation to their overall word counts see Natalie Hanna, 'Gender and Social Status in Chaucer's Language' (unpublished doctoral thesis, University of Liverpool, 2016), 55–56.
6. Kim M. Phillips, *Medieval Maidens: Young Women and Gender in England, 1270–1540* (Manchester: Manchester University Press, 2003).
7. Geoffrey Chaucer, "The Merchant's Tale," in *The Riverside Chaucer,* ed. Larry D. Benson (Oxford: Oxford University Press, 2008), 1311–1315 (referred to by line number in this edition).
8. Ibid., 1418, 1419, 1420, 1422.
9. Ibid., 1359, 1288, 1291, 1324, 1379, 1376.
10. Ibid., 1271, 1515, 1557.
11. Ibid., 1252, 1416, 1432.
12. Phillips, *Medieval Maidens,* 45–47.
13. Chaucer, "Merchant's Tale," 1424–1425.
14. Hallissy, "Widow-To-Be," 296.
15. Ibid., 297–298.
16. Chaucer, "Merchant's Tale," 1429.
17. Ibid., 1270.
18. Peggy Knapp, *Chaucer and the Social Contest* (New York: Routledge, 1990), 108.
19. Chaucer, "Merchant's Tale," 2135.
20. Ibid., 2138–2148: "Rise up my wife, my love, my lady free! The garden is enclosed all around; come forth my pure spouse! Beyond doubt, you have wounded me in my heart, O wife! … I chose you to be my wife and my solace." All translations are my own.
21. Ibid., 2087.
22. Ibid., 2091.
23. Ibid., 2138.
24. Ibid., 2160, 2164.
25. Ibid., 2184.
26. Ibid., 1268, 1271, 1305, 1445, 1447, 1515, 1531.
27. Frances McSparren et al., eds., "The Middle English Dictionary Online," accessed 26 March 2015, http://quod.lib.umich.edu/m/med/lookup.html. See definition 2a. For additional negative connotations see 1d, 3a, and 4a and also, Michael Proffitt et al., eds., *The Oxford English Dictionary Online,* http://www.oed.com. See definition II.
28. McSparren et al., eds., "The Middle English Dictionary Online."
29. Elizabeth Simmons-O'Neill, "Love in Hell: The Role of Pluto and Proserpine in Chaucer's *Merchant's Tale,*" *Modern Language Quarterly: A Journal of Literary History* 51, no. 3 (1990): 392.
30. Chaucer, "Merchant's Tale," 1260, 1344, 1370, 1389.
31. See 1 Samuel 25. Note especially 25: 36–38.
32. Ibid., 1228, 1255, 1283, 1405, 1546, 1651, 1663, 1666, 1731. See also Geoffrey Chaucer, The Clerk's Tale," in Benson, *The Riverside Chaucer,* 137–152, at lines 111, 622, 1180. See also, Geoffrey Chaucer, "The Shipman's Tale," in Benson, *The Riverside Chaucer,* 203–208, at line 103.
33. Chaucer, "Merchant's Tale," 1253–1257: "Whether it was for religious reasons or senility, I cannot say, but this knight had such a great desire to be a wedded man that day and night he would do all he could to find out how to become wedded."

34. Geoffrey Chaucer, "The Franklin's Tale," in Benson, *The Riverside Chaucer*, 179–189, at line 709.
35. Chaucer, "Merchant's Tale," 1254.
36. Proffitt, et al., *The Oxford English Dictionary Online*.
37. Chaucer, "Merchant's Tale," 1458–1459.
38. Hallissy, "Widow-To-Be," 302.
39. Chaucer, "Shipman's Tale," 100–103: "'Niece,'" he said, "Five hours should be sufficient for a night's sleep, unless it were for an old feeble creature, as these wedded men are, that lie and doze."
40. Chaucer, "Clerk's Tale," 109–111.
41. Ibid., 1180–1182: "No wedded man should be so bold as to test his wife's patience and expect to find Griselda's, for he shall certainly fail."
42. Ibid., 733.
43. Ibid., 622–623.
44. Chaucer, "Merchant's Tale," 1223–1225.
45. Chaucer, "Clerk's Tale," 1191.
46. Ibid., 135.
47. Ibid., 800–801.
48. Simmons-O'Neill, "Love in Hell," 394–395.

Chapter 6

Objectification, Empowerment, and the Male Gaze in the Lanval Corpus

Elizabeth S. Leet

Two Middle English Breton lays—the anonymous mid-fourteenth-century *Sir Landevale* and Thomas Chestre's late fourteenth-century *Sir Launfal*—present adaptations of Marie de France's mid-twelfth-century *lai de Lanval*, a tale that, in its original, demonstrates an alternative to the courtly femininity of much medieval verse. The fairy women who love Lanval, Landevale, and Launfal rescue them from financial ruin, save them from accusations of homosexuality, and spirit them away on the backs of white palfreys.[1] By using their wealth, courtly animals, and physical beauty to free their lovers, each fairy mistress participates actively in the male gaze and circumvents the social expectations levied on many courtly women. Although the male gaze has often been cited as a sign of the visual dominance male onlookers exert on female bodies, the fairy monarchs carefully design their powerful physical entities in order to liberate their chosen consorts and retreat to their private fairy realms.

Opposite the posturing machinations and prideful lust of Guinevere, the fairies embody economic and social independence when they arrive in Arthur's court. Their presence is a flash in the pan. They arrive and disappear with equal economy of both language and action, and yet the mere suggestion of their existence whips Guinevere, King Arthur, and the entire court into a frenzy of bruised egos and thwarted judicial proceedings. I argue that these fairy women embody the desire of each eponymous knight, whose potent male gaze seems to imagine each beautiful benefactor into existence. Concurrently, the fairy ladies also style themselves with rich clothing and courtly animals to attract the gazes of townspeople and Arthurian courtiers alike, maximizing their scopophilic impact in order to liberate their lover.

Male scopophilic desire demands a female object. The film theorist Laura Mulvey establishes the projection of active male desire onto passive female bodies on the silver screen. She explains that a female character, "stands in patriarchal culture as signifier for the male other, bound by a symbolic order in which man can live out his fantasies and obsessions ... by imposing them on the silent image of woman still tied to her place as bearer of meaning, not maker of meaning."[2] Likewise in literature, onlookers may project desire onto an object or objects. In the Lanval corpus, onlookers of different social classes, genders, and ages assess a fairy or group of fairies on the basis of their idealized courtly femininity, and each fairy styles her body according to which gaze—either public or private—she will receive. Each fairy participates in the male scopophilic fantasy by modifying her attire and the animals around her in order to create an optimized image that, like physical evidence, will resolve her lover's legal troubles.

The intersection between empowerment and objectification inherent in this portrait of the gaze characterizes every text in the Lanval corpus. Descriptions of each fairy's physical appearance and her luxurious garments, as well as the animals surrounding her, lend texture, depth, and meaning to her body, recalling Donna Haraway's posthumanist constructions of female identity,[3] and allude to her wealth and courtly mannerisms. Instead of focusing solely on her sexual body, the gaze also scans the animals she brings to emphasize wealth, autonomy, courtliness, and nobility. While each poet delineates his or her fairy's relationship to horses, hunting dogs, and falcons, the descriptions become increasingly static with each successive adaptation. As the ladies and their animals move and interact less, their assemblage seems increasingly designed for visual consumption.

Marie, the *Landevale* poet, and Chestre—in conjunction with the male gaze that pervades the Lanval corpus—describe fairies who are physically beautiful, richly attired, and surrounded by expensive animals. The male juridical and royal onlookers, combined with their visibility to voyeurs of all genders, social classes, and ages while traveling to Arthur's throne room, point to the fundamental *"to-be-looked-at-ness"*[4] of each fairy, and she comes to embody both the desire of those who look at her and her own need to liberate her embattled beloved. As a calculated response to the threat of her lover's conviction, each fairy carefully styles her body to achieve maximum visual impact and prove his innocence. Indeed, despite her agency as her beloved's benefactor and savior, each fairy's body becomes the physical evidence of the veracity of her lover's claims. Her objectification, therefore, is inextricably linked with her autonomy.

Lanval

In the original lay, we meet Lanval, an Arthurian knight who fails to receive his inheritance due to circumstances outside his control.[5] Frustrated and nearly penniless, Lanval leaves court in a hurry, taking only his horse—his only possession and the last remaining symbol of his chivalric status. Lanval then arrives in a supernatural valley bisected by a river where his mount immediately collapses, overtaken by mystical forces, and he is left horseless and without recourse against his destitution. The horse in *Lanval* becomes a crucial barometer for the supernatural elements in the environment just as it foreshadows the subsequent connection between the fairy and her horse when she enters Arthur's throne room. Two fairies arrive, summoned by the supernatural crisis the horse experiences in the valley, and bring Lanval to their fairy mistress, who has loved him from afar. Though his fairy mistress demands that their love remain secret, Lanval betrays her existence when Guinevere confronts him with unwanted sexual advances. At the mere suggestion that any woman might be more beautiful than she, Guinevere quickly denounces Lanval as a homosexual,[6] provoking an enormous scandal at court.[7] Lanval then spends the duration of the tale in a precarious position, one necessary to demonstrate for both Arthur's court and the reader the superior political, financial, and scopophilic power of his fairy beloved.[8]

After Lanval rejects Guinevere, the Arthurian judicial proceedings commence, overseen by none other than Arthur himself. Lanval must then produce evidence of his fairy. In this final scene, Marie provides her reader with a *deus ex machina*: the sudden appearance of a cohort of ladies and their fairy leader, exactly the persons required to resolve the judicial matter.[9] She becomes the ideal object of the male gaze, a gaze that, simply by existing and desiring, forces an object to materialize. As A. C. Spearing argues: "the lady consciously displays herself as a sight, moving slowly and wearing what will reveal enough of her beauty to stimulate the imagination to supply what is unseen; the description is detailed enough to amount to a formal *effictio*.[10] The effect is such as to imply that the lady *wishes* to be fragmented by the onlookers' eyes, wishes that each of her parts should be fetishized as a means to power."[11] She is objectified and powerful, consumed by voyeurs in her diegetic environment in order to accomplish her goal of freeing Lanval. In addition to Spearing's argument that she desires power, I suggest she desires Lanval and uses her political, economic, sartorial, and visual power to rescue him. The fairy leader does not conform to Mulvey's schema, where "the male protagonist is free to command the stage, a stage of spatial illusion in which he articulates the look and creates the action."[12] Although the men at court visually consume her flesh, she first catches them in her web, overturning the aesthetic hierarchy in which Guinevere was thought to be superior and taking her chosen consort away into her land.

Moreover, the way horses facilitate fairy movement distinguishes these supernatural women from Guinevere, who wields influence only in the limited indoor spaces of her husband's castle. Conversely, the fairy lady's damsels rescue Lanval in response to the collapse of his horse and, later, all the fairies arrive in Arthur's court on the backs of superlative equine specimens. In Marie's *Lanval*, the ladies and palfreys constitute fluid entities: descriptions of one run into descriptions of the other as flanks, golden hair, and beautiful faces are juxtaposed across species.[13] Each description of the fairy mistress reveals shared movement whereby she and her animal entourage interact with each other as they enter Arthur's throne room. The fairy rides her palfrey [*"chevalchot"* (v. 557)] who, in turn, carries her gently [*"ki bien e suëf la portot"* (v. 558)]. Her hunting dog also follows her [*"aprés li vint"* (v. 580)] instead of appearing statically at her side as in the later adaptations. Each animal moves in concert with the fairy mistress to approach the throne and free Lanval. Although the fairy damsels and their leader present a different femininity from that of Guinevere, their otherness does not beget wildness: the fairy ladies demonstrate exemplary courtly manners and receive universal and immediate acclaim.

By bonding silently and effortlessly with her palfrey and hunting dog, Lanval's fairy asserts power outside the humanistic limitations of verbal language or patriarchal politics, all while revealing her mastery of courtly manners and control of hunting animals. When the fairy enters Arthur's throne room in the final scene of her tale, the narrator glides from descriptions of harnesses and equipment directly to dresses and flesh to establish interspecies bonds as a source of the fairy's strength, even evoking the horse-goddess Epona, a popular deity revered in Celtic mythological traditions.[14] The fairy mistress acts as a knight in this scene: her bold arrival expresses both her wealth and autonomy, just as it displays an aesthetic ideal and troubles any supposition that power resides in a human, male, singular body. Instead, agency is fairy, female, and plural. Marie's throng of fairies defy the patriarchal[15] court and exploit the covetous male gaze.

In *Lanval*, however, those who gaze are not always male. In particular, Lanval feels the gaze on his body when lustful Queen Guinevere attempts to seduce him. As soon as Guinevere propositions him, Lanval reneges on his solemn vow to protect his mistress's anonymity. He invokes his lover's beauty—stating that even the fairy's lowliest chambermaid is lovelier than Guinevere[16]—in order to escape Guinevere's objectifying, predatory gaze. As a result, his masculinity and his courtliness come under the Arthurian microscope.

Lanval finds himself between two women: one who inflicts the gaze upon him and another who voluntarily becomes objectified for her benefit.

He must navigate between the Scylla of Guinevere's loquacious and predatory sexuality and the Charybdis of the fairy mistress's mystical and silent femininity. Speech, therefore, reveals many of Marie's subversions of gender norms. In her book *Bodytalk: When Women Speak in Old French Literature,* E. Jane Burns makes a similar argument about Chrétien's Enide, another woman often observed and silent: "We begin to see how the objectification of the lovely lady, so crucial to the working of the courtly milieu, where she provides the inspiration for feats of prowess, the audience for chivalric combat, and the supportive listener for tales of adventure, focuses principally on the female body. The heroine's speech more staunchly resists colonization and appropriation; her constructed voice cannot be fetishized as easily as her fictive flesh."[17] Chivalric tales frequently refigure this objectification and commodification of female characters. By focusing on the female body as the woman's principal sphere of influence over and above her speech or actions, the Lanval corpus is partisan to similar gender troubles. Burns examines this phenomenon of reducing medieval female literary characters to sensual and silent bodies. Her term "bodytalk" refers to the nonverbal language wielded by female characters in the absence of affording them the discursive speech monopolized by their male counterparts. Likewise, the tales of the Lanval corpus locate their fairy mistresses' influence within the limits of their own bodies and the multiple materials, textures, colors, jewels, and animals that adorn them.

These tales reveal visually alluring fairy ladies who nevertheless upend the structure and stricture of the gaze by reclaiming their objectification for their own ends. The Lanval myth resists the notion that the object of the male gaze is always fundamentally and negatively objectified. These fairies demonstrate prowess outside speech. By taking advantage of their own physical beauty and the opulent materials that complement it, the fairy women liberate their consorts and retreat victorious into fairyland. By reappropriating their bodies for their own purposes, they defy the colonizing power of the male gaze and of its practitioners.

Because Marie presents fairies as physical evidence in a judicial proceeding, she forces us—as well as her subsequent Middle English adapters—to consider the implications of her bifurcated characterization of female autonomy and objectification. As we will see, the *Landevale* poet's anonymous fairy lover and Chestre's Dame Tryamour hold Arthur's court in thrall by submitting their extensively styled bodies to visual evaluation by townspeople and courtiers alike. Indeed, the *Landevale* poet and Chestre each valorize courtly social mores over mythological Celtic content. While expanding the influence of the Lanval story across non-French territories, these Middle English versions also render their female protagonists more visual and more verbose. While the silence of their parent text presents a compelling analog to Burns's female "bodytalk" and situates female-equine relationships at its core, the fairies in *Sir Landevale* and *Sir Launfal* capitalize on the courtly currencies of sartorial opulence and discursive speech.

Landevale and Launfal

The two significant adaptations of *Lanval* are the anonymous fourteenth-century Middle English *Sir Landevale*[18] and Thomas Chestre's late fourteenth-century *Sir Launfal*.[19] Spearing suggests that *Sir Landevale* represents an intermediate, though perhaps superficial, revisiting of Marie's lay, transcribing her original stylistic, narrative, and thematic content into a new language and context.[20] He attributes the loss of emotional interiority and delicate subtext to the linguistic shift from Old French to Middle English, a transition difficult (or perhaps impossible) to effectuate without losing some of the grammatical and lexical particularities that contribute to Marie's stylistic subtlety.[21] I argue, however, that Marie's adapters minimize emotional interiority in order to reorient the tale around the fairies' self-styling to attract public and private gazes. The materialism that characterizes both adaptations reflects the century of their creation: with the renewed literary interest in the Breton lay genre, fourteenth-century poets like the *Landevale* poet and Thomas Chestre adapted and altered Marie's original in exactly the places ripe for material elaboration.[22] Both Middle English poets detail the garments and courtly animals that surround their respective fairy queens in order to appeal to a wider audience.

Although the fairies in the adaptations lose mystical power as they become courtlier, the *Landevale* poet and Chestre present female protagonists who gain stereotypically male political power when they enter a foreign court. While less mysterious, they are not less powerful. Still, as with Marie's original fairy, we must interrogate their power because of the problematic gaze-centered means through which they wield it.

Both adaptations certainly linger on this ambiguity. While the fairy ladies in each adaptation speak more than Marie's fairy queen, they still express no opinions nor do they articulate their own emotions. These women, while lacking the self-reflexivity afforded to many protagonists in the Arthurian tradition, also move away from the mystical independence that characterizes the fairies of Marie's original. The *Landevale* poet and Chestre keep their versions of Marie's autonomous ladies firmly in the political realm. In Marie's *Lanval*, the paucity of female speech belies the supernatural power within these women, whereas her Middle English adapters write ladies whose verbosity renders their intervention courtly and accessible. The ladies of *Sir Landevale* and *Sir Launfal* experience reduced interiority in favor of outward displays of verbal, human agency.[23]

In Arthur's throne room, both *Sir Landevale* and *Sir Launfal* assume an anthropocentric perspective demonstrated by the decreased participation of nonhuman animals. Although this is the second climactic moment when horses play a key role, the *Landevale* poet minimizes the unity of the horse-woman pair. Unlike the original *Lanval*, *Sir Landevale*'s horses do not become a part of the fairy's identity: she associates with horses without being defined by her relationship to the equine.[24] Instead, three white greyhounds follow her as she sits passively astride her smooth-trotting palfrey ["A softe paas her palfrey comaunde" (v. 448)]; all the while a sparrowhawk rests on her hand. Her interactions with nonhuman animals become more superficial than those of the fairy lady in *Lanval*. She is merely on her palfrey ["On a white palfrey comlye" (v. 427)] instead of riding him actively like Marie's fairy lady, though the horse is far more expensive than his predecessor: no king could afford such a horse without selling lands to cover the cost ["There nesse kyng that hath gold ne fee / That myght by that palfrey / Withoute sellyng of lond awey" (vv. 428–430)]. The fairy mistress in *Sir Landevale*, therefore, becomes increasingly privileged and passive.

The *Landevale* poet also expands the existing tradition of metaphors evoking adornment to emphasize the signs of wealth and courtliness layered on and surrounding the fairy queen's body. He adapts and deepens this topos from Marie's *Lanval*, in which the woman's neck is whiter than snow on a branch ["*le col plus blanc que neif sur branche*" (v. 570)]. The *Landevale* poet compares her to a blossom on a briar ["blossome on brere" (v. 431)] and to a gentle bird alighting on a branch ["Jentylle and jolyffe as birde on bowgh" (v. 433)], detailing her bejeweled crown placed atop her metallic golden hair ["As gold wyre yn sonn bright" (v. 437)], her pale purple cloak, her narrow waist, and the delicately folded arms that show her shapely figure to its best advantage ["Whiche wel becam that lady" (v. 445)]. The *Sir Landevale* fairy lady presents herself to maximize her assets: the beautiful features, rich clothing, and expensive courtly animals appear like adornments on a body that, in turn, embellishes and complements male knighthood.

The proliferation of textural details and allusions to adornment invite the attention and desire of the men at Arthur's court. By mixing velvet and sparrowhawk feathers, a palfrey's sleek coat and the fairy's tendrils of golden hair, the poet imbricates her fairy *to-be-looked-at-ness* with what I call a *to-be-touched-ness*. The visual and the haptic become enmeshed as the onlookers are incited to desire the fairy. To resolve the personal-turned-judicial matter of whether the fairy or Guinevere is more beautiful, the fairy enters herself as physical evidence by which the whole town, all the courtiers, and even Guinevere herself, may judge her physical appearance ["Throw the citie rode she, / For every man shuld hir see. / Wiff and childe, yong and olde, / Al come hir to byholde." (vv. 449–452)]. The poet insists on her visibility to all and suggests the visual impact of her body summons onlookers to appear just as her self-styling invites their assessment. Expanding Mulvey's male scopophilic power, *Sir Landevale* and *Sir Launfal* point to the many genders and classes of gazers who watch the fairies ride through the city, including barons, peasants, women, and children. The fairy leader accepts the gaze as the only means by which she can free her lover and surrenders temporarily to visual dissection by all onlookers, not simply those participating in the trial. The universal admiration of those who gaze upon her resolves the debate at court over the relative beauty of the fairy and mortal women, while also establishing the fairy mistress as a visual ideal that onlookers of all social classes, genders, and ages may use to judge women. Like Mulvey's argument that mainstream film codes the erotic into the languages of the dominant patriarchal order, these diverse onlookers effectuate a starkly monolithic, male, heterosexual, and objectifying gaze.[25] All who look at the fairies are subsumed into the same vortex of male scopophilia.

In turn, *Sir Landevale*'s fairy mistress functions simultaneously as *deus ex machina* and the embodiment of the objectification she undergoes to confirm her superlative beauty.[26] Her visibility is fundamentally linked to her role as the savior, the knight on a white horse who rescues her beloved. As Spearing argues, this myth is one of wish fulfillment, where ladies mystically arrive to rescue men in need.[27] However, while the *Landevale* poet's fairy materializes at the moment of knightly desperation—suggesting that female characters act as fantasies that respond directly to the desires of their male counterparts—she also uses this moment of salvation to seduce the man she loves and, later, to bring him into her land as her consort. It is, therefore, both Landevale and his fairy mistress whose desires are sated and whose wishes are fulfilled.

In *Sir Launfal,* Chestre inserts the fairy intervention at the exact moment when Guinevere speaks to Arthur about Launfal's brazen assertion. Dame Tryamour's public arrival directly answers the public accusations against Launfal ["The barouns seygh come rydynge / A damesele alone / Upoon a whyt comely palfrey" (vv. 926–928)]. The barons, also referencing the judicial nature of this testimony, then produce—via the narrator's description—a picture of her body and dress, cinematically scanning her up and down, the "camera"[28] assessing her every curve and the signs and symbols of her status.[29]

The gaze starts at her head and travels down her body. It moves then to her delicate figure and tiny waist ["Wyth gentyll body and myddyll small, / That semely was of syght" (vv. 944–945)] and the ermine trim on her cloak ["Her mantyll was furryd wyth whyt ermyn, / Yreversyd jolyf and fyn" (vv. 946–947)]. Chestre describes her gold saddle adorned with gold bells as universally coveted ["Her sadell was semyly set: / The sambus wer grene felvet / Ypaynted wyth ymagerye. / The bordure was of belles / Of ryche gold, and nothing elles / That any man myghte aspye. / In the arsouns, before and behynde, / Were twey stones of Ynde, / Gay for the maystrye" (vv. 949–957)]. The saddle is not the only adornment on the fairy's palfrey, whose breastplate alone is worth an earldom ["The paytrelle of her palfraye / Was worth an erldome, stoute and gay. / The best yn Lumbardye" (vv. 958–960)]. Despite the heavy, jewel-encrusted tack her horse wears, the palfrey carries his rider into court at an easy pace so she may be seen to advantage ["A softe pas her palfray fond / That men her schuld beholde" (vv. 962–963)]. The bodies of the fairy and her palfrey evoke ease and wealth in their every detail and adornment. Chestre uses metaphors of embellishment like those in *Sir Landevale* to insist on the fairy's ability to capture male scopophilic attention.

Yet despite certain shared metaphors, Chestre further reduces the fairy's agency by listing her accoutrements without a single active verb to describe her relationship to them. Her courtly animals come last as the final set pieces of this fairy assemblage. The falcon perched on her hand ["A gerfawcon sche bar on her hond" (v. 961)], the greyhounds in gold collars who trot alongside her ["Twey whyte grehoundys ronne hyr by— / Har colers were of golde" (vv. 965–966)] and the other nonhuman accessories serve only to identify her, to make her rich without enriching her. Like *Sir Landevale*, a parallel appears between the falcon perched on her delicate wrist and Tryamour seated gently atop her horse. Interaction between the beings in this courtly tableau only appears at the end of Chestre's description, when only one verb describes their shared movement ["Thorugh Karlyon rood that lady" (v. 964)]. Dame Tryamour becomes even more passive than the *Landevale* fairy in relation to the male voyeurs' active desire. Still, despite their different degrees of fairy passivity, Landevale's fairy mistress and Launfal's Dame Tryamour are surrounded with such adornment as to limit their interaction with animals and nearly eclipse them altogether.

Styling for the Gaze

Although fairy women are unambiguously objectified in these three versions of the Lanval myth, each poet presents his or her fairy mistress as an active participant in the self-embellishment that captivates onlookers. Each fairy carefully styles herself, selecting her clothing and those animals around her to maximize her visual impact upon arrival at court. Similar shifts in fairy attire from the tent to the Arthurian trial demonstrate the fairies' deliberate but temporary acceptance of their own objectification. Each poet reveals a marked difference in appearance, setting, and attire between each fairy's first meeting with her lover and her subsequent entry into Arthur's court.

All three fairies style themselves provocatively and strategically show their bodies for their first meeting with the beloved knight each woman has summoned to her opulent woodland tent.[30] In Marie's original *Lanval*, the contrast between flesh, fabric, and ermine characterizes the fairy's impact on both Lanval and the listener.[31] Marie's fairy reclines on a bed whose sheets alone are as expensive as a castle ["*li drap valeient un chastel*" (v. 98)]. She wears only her shirt to show her fine figure ["*Mult ot le cors bien fait e gent*" (v. 100)] and drapes a mantle of fine Alexandrine ermine across herself ["*Un chier mantel de blanc hermine, / covert de purpre Alexandrine, / ot pur le chalt sur li geté*" (vv. 101–103)]. The curves of her hips appear from under the mantle and tunic, and her face, neck, and chest are whiter than hawthorn blooms ["*tut ot descovert le costé, / le vis, le col e la peitrine: / plus ert blanche que flurs d'espine*" (vv. 104–106)]. The juxtaposition of fur with flesh highlights the dichotomy between expensive courtly materials and the sensual woman who wears them to seduce the man she has loved from afar.

Marie introduces these key markers of both wealth and sensuality that recur in *Sir Landevale* and *Sir Launfal*. Landevale's fairy mistress also appears almost naked on a rich bed, wrapped in an ermine mantle.[32] *Sir Launfal*, likewise, exploits the same titillating imagery of fair skin only partly covered by luxurious furs.[33] Each fairy styles herself to captivate Lanval, Landevale, or Launfal according to a particularly sexual and private iteration of the male gaze. In the tent, the fairy lady seduces her mortal lover by pulling the focus to her flesh, prefiguring the scrutiny of Arthur's courtiers. The change occurs when the onlookers multiply. As the solution to the judicial threat, each fairy lady must maximize her body's visual impact in the public judicial sphere.

Throughout the Lanval corpus, women and their animals facilitate chivalric action and patriarchal political upheaval while choosing to participate in a system of visual colonization by male onlookers. The fairy ladies and Dame Tryamour arrive with full *cortège* to save their beloved knights from their judicial predicaments, therefore submitting tacitly to be entered into evidence in their own right. The fairies style themselves deliberately to facilitate the Arthurian courtiers' dissection of each part of their body and entourage, from the commodified signposts of their courtly beauty to the ornate equipage of their palfreys. Each poet modifies the supernatural, courtly, sartorial, and animal materialities of the fairy lady to attract attention not only to her body, clothing, and animals but to the dialectical movement between fairy styling and the mass of onlookers who watch and judge her, one that inspires the adapters and that permits each fairy to retreat into fairyland. Adaptations of Marie's original inscribe this exchange into a pattern of materialist adjustments that connects each tale to the audience, time period, and society in which it was written. In particular, as the Middle English ladies become less supernatural and gain more wealth and autonomy, they bear witness to the expanded social roles afforded to fourteenth-century women.

One might claim that, once each of these three fairy ladies send envoys to fetch Lanval, Landevale, and Launfal, they forgo the independence they enjoy in their secluded fairy realms. This, I believe, would be a mistake. The agency of each fairy mistress reorients not toward the imperiled Lanval, judicial proceedings, or styled femininity, but toward her own selection of a romantic partner and her decision to rescue him. Each fairy falls in love and brings her partner with her into fairyland, where she is visible only to the gaze of her lover. The conclusion of each tale confirms the temporary nature of each fairy lady's surrender to male voyeuristic assessment and reiterates her acceptance of objectification in exchange for love.

Each tale in the Lanval corpus interrogates the oppositions between objectification and empowerment, between the one who wishes and the one who fulfills that wish. Criticism of these tales has seen the fairy mistresses as objectified by male voyeurs and as an answer to the needs of their beloved knights, lacking agency in their own right. This assumption is reasonable considering the women in many medieval tales who submit to men and to male demands, but the Lanval tales do not permit the facile resolution of the contradictions they expose. Each fairy lady is both objectified and empowered. Each fairy rescues a destitute knight stranded in a mystical valley, gives him money, and helps him avoid a conviction at trial even after he violates her sole request. Yet, while her aid serves his purposes, she also actively pursues him, uses her exorbitant wealth and physical beauty to ensure a future with the man she loves, and finally takes him into her own fairy kingdom as her consort. The Lanval myths conclude at this moment of retreat from the mortal world, as the temporary object of the male gaze takes her prize into fairyland, disappearing from our view forever. In these tales, one moment of objectification buys each fairy an eternity of independence with her beloved, a trade-off that obscures the distinction between those who gaze and those who are gazed upon, the agent and the object, the wish and its fulfillment.

Acknowledgments

This article was made possible by the Phi Beta Kappa Society's Mary Isabel Sibley Award for research in France.

Elizabeth S. Leet is Assistant Professor of French at Washington & Jefferson College.

Notes

1. Sharon Kinoshita traces feminist readings of *Lanval* and posits the reversal of gender as a sort of female Cinderella story in "Cherchez la femme: Feminist Criticism and Marie de France's *Lai de Lanval*," *Romance Notes* 34, no. 3 (1994): 263–273.
2. Laura Mulvey, "Visual Pleasure and Narrative Cinema," *Screen* 16, no. 3 (1975): 199.
3. For more on female bodily hybridity, see Haraway's *Simians, Cyborgs, and Women: The Reinvention of Nature* (New York: Routledge, 1991); for discussion of interspecies language relevant to the Lanval corpus's relationships between women, hawks, hounds, and palfreys, see her *When Species Meet* (Minneapolis: University of Minnesota Press, 2007).
4. Mulvey, "Visual Pleasure and Narrative Cinema," 203.
5. Marie de France, *Lanval*, in *Lais*, ed. A. Ewert and Glyn S. Burgess (London: Bristol Classical, 1995).
6. Among medievalists, the most common terminology for Guinevere's accusation is to say she denounces Lanval as a homosexual, despite the anachronistic use of the term. The first use of the term homosexual is in an 1869 anonymous German pamphlet opposing a Prussian anti-sodomy law. This appearance was

soon echoed in Gustav Jager's *Discovery of the Soul* (1880) and then in Richard von Krafft-Ebing's *Psychopathia Sexualis* (1886). For more on the evolution of homosexuality since Ancient Greece, see David M. Halperin's *One Hundred Years of Homosexuality* (New York: Routledge, 1990).

7. Didier Godard links the Christian stigmatization of male homosexual desire and practice to the spiritual imperative to oppose pagan sodomy. Despite *Lanval*'s decidedly secular context, it is important to note the extreme religious and political consequences that would have been levied by the society in which Marie penned her tale. Lanval's easy exoneration would not have been likely outside the realms of fiction and fantasy. See Godard, *Deux hommes sur un cheval: L'Homosexualité masculine au Moyen Âge* (Béziers, France: H&O éditions, 2003), 104.
8. Tison Pugh, *Sexuality and Its Queer Discontents in Middle English Literature* (New York: Palgrave MacMillan, 2008), 1.
9. We must note that the judicial proceedings constitute a much graver consequence for Lanval than Guinevere's accusation of homosexuality. Godard explains the tolerance of homosexual acts beginning in the early eleventh century that led to, "widespread homosexuality, easily and peacefully experienced, in an atmosphere that was quite different from that which we might imagine to exist in the European Christian Middle Ages ("une homosexualité répandue, facilement et tranquillement vécue, dans une atmosphère assez différente de celle que nous pourrions imaginer, a priori, s'agissant de l'Europe chrétienne au Moyen Âge") However, the twelfth century ushered in new social and political restructuring that forced homosexuals to the margins of society as social or cultural outsiders. He states, "More and more, over the course of the following centuries, homosexuality came to be perceived, not perhaps without reason ..., as dangerous for the established order and social hierarchy" ("De plus en plus, au cours des siècles suivants, l'homosexualité sera pareillement perçue, non peut-être sans raison ..., comme dangereuse pour l'ordre établi et la hiérarchie sociale"). The implied but unstated homosexuality of Landevale and Launfal, therefore, would carry a more severe resonance. See Godard, *Deux hommes*, 99 and 103.
10. Although Sarah Bernthal omits Lanval's fairy lady from her study, her *effictio* may be understood as an elective dismemberment of her body to maximize its visual impact. See Berthal's "Dismemberment and Remembrance in the Lais of Marie de France," *Pacific Coast Philology* 54, no. 1 (2019): 20–37.
11. A. C. Spearing, "The Lanval Story," in *The Medieval Poet as Voyeur: Looking and Listening in Medieval Love-narratives* (Cambridge: Cambridge University Press, 1993), 102.
12. Mulvey, "Visual Pleasure and Narrative Cinema," 204.
13. Marie de France, *Lanval*, vv. 553–580.
14. Miranda Green provides useful understanding of the zoomorphic hybridity between Epona and her horse(s), which relates to the characterization of the fairy ladies—notably in the original *Lanval*—as inseparable from their mounts. See Green, *Animals in Celtic Life and Myth* (London: Routledge, 1992), 204–210. Jean Markale, on the other hand, insists upon the otherworldly qualities the Celts saw in horses which allowed them to travel, bringing with them a rider, between the human world and a fairy realm in *La femme celte: mythe et sociologie* (Paris: Payot, 1972), 76.

15. Jane Chance discusses the masculinist portrayal of Arthurian society in *Lanval*. See "Marie de France Versus King Arthur: Lanval's Gender Inversion as Breton Subversion," in Chance, *The Literary Subversions of Medieval Women* (New York: Palgrave Macmillan, 2007), 45.
16. Marie de France, *Lanval*, vv. 322–326.
17. E. Jane Burns, "Rewriting Men's Stories: Enide's Disruptive Mouths," in Burns, *Bodytalk: When Women Speak in Old French Literature* (Philadelphia: University of Pennsylvania, 1993), 158.
18. *Sir Landevale*, in *The Middle English Breton Lays*, ed. Anne Laskaya and Eve Salisbury (Kalamazoo, MI: Medieval Institute Publications, 1995), 423–437.
19. Thomas Chestre, *Sir Launfal*, in *The Middle English Breton Lays*, 201–262.
20. A. C. Spearing, "Marie de France and Her Middle English Adapters," *Studies in the Age of Chaucer* 12 (1990): 118.
21. Myra Seaman, "Thomas Chestre's Sir Launfal and the Englishing of Medieval Romance," *Medieval Perspectives* 15 (2000): 106.
22. Timothy D. O'Brien discusses fourteenth-century interest in Breton lays as a literary genre as the reason for their adaptation two hundred years after Marie's original (34–35). See "The 'Readerly' Sir Launfal," *Parergon* 8, no. 1 (1990): 33–45. In addition, Myra Seaman explains that the different audience for the late medieval English adaptations influences their poets' decision to explore the materials that distinguish characters (109).
23. One important shift in the verbal content of the tales occurs between *Sir Landevale* and *Sir Launfal*. In the latter, Guinevere is permitted to speak at trial.
24. *Sir Landevale*, vv. 423–448.
25. Mulvey, "Visual Pleasure and Narrative Cinema," 200.
26. Laskaya and Salisbury, *Breton Lays*, 206.
27. A. C. Spearing, "Marie de France and Her Middle English Adapters," 118.
28. Mulvey discusses the relationship between women, their clothing, and the gaze by using the character "Lisa" in Hitchcock's *Rear Window*. She argues that Lisa, much like the fairy ladies of the Lanval tradition, becomes a "passive image of visual perfection." She is both eager to be seen, via the inversion of scopophilic tendencies by which one enjoys watching, and also made available for visual consumption by participating in her boyfriend's voyeuristic life. In "Visual Pleasure and Narrative Cinema," 206–207.
29. Thomas Chestre, *Sir Launfal*, vv. 929–966.
30. Spearing discusses this episode of self-display and the power she wields by commanding the gaze in "The Lanval Story," 100–101.
31. Marie de France, *Lanval*, vv. 97–106.
32. *Sir Landevale*, vv. 91–106.
33. Thomas Chestre, *Sir Launfal*, vv. 277–294.

Chapter 7

Pueri Sunt Pueri
Machismo, Chivalry, and the Aggressive Pastimes of the Medieval Male Youth

Sean McGlynn

In practice, medieval chivalry, despite the popular image of fair maidens in distress, served the needs of men rather than women. Chivalry was, first and foremost, a manifestation of a martial ethos; fashions, courtly love and purported consideration for women were very much secondary embellishments.[1] It is this martial ethos that guided the aggressive past-times of male youths. Here I explore how much of the phenomenon of chivalry "at play" was mere machismo posturing and how much was serious training for the business of war. The place of the tournament—the apogee of such entertainments as a form of medieval war games within a violent sports spectacle—will play a central role in the overall analysis. "Boys will be boys" (the Latin "pueri sunt pueri" is literally "boys are boys") had a very serious application that was actively encouraged by society and state controls. However, the preparation for this both through boys' play and the more mature pursuit of hunting also deserve consideration to explicate further the aggressive world of male bonding and the role of the tournament in an age where male martial values predominated.

We have today a clichéd picture of medieval times as being incredibly brutal. At the opening of the International War Crimes Tribunal at The Hague in 2002, Carla del Ponte, the chief prosecutor, accused Slobodan Milosevic of "medieval barbarity."[2] But the sad fact is there is much truth in this cliché.[3] The pervasive presence of war in medieval society helped to nurture an environment in which violence permeated culture and society. As Philippe Contamine has rightly observed, medieval war is decisive "as an explanatory factor and as the product of a whole cultural, technical and economic environment."[4] Combine this with the testosterone surges of male adolescence and one would expect to see aggression manifesting itself in their play and upbringing.

Examples of this are plentiful. In early thirteenth-century England, the chronicler Roger of Wendover informs us of quintessential expressions of male-bonding among youth: serious crowd violence at a football match and a wrestling match in London that erupted into full-scale rioting, resulting in widespread damage to property, for which the ringleader was hanged and his chief cohorts had their hands and feet amputated.[5] It is not surprising that the original name for football was campball, with camp deriving from the Latin *campus*, denoting not just an open field but also, with more gladiatorial connotations, the field of battle.[6] As in this last event, violence was not so often the result of a sporting event, but rather its raison d'être, as a couple of examples demonstrate: one medieval game involved the chasing of a pig by men with clubs, the fun being in beating the animal to death; in another, a live cat was nailed to a post while competitors attempted head-butting it to death. Bear- and bull-baiting were also staples.[7]

It hardly needs a moment's reflection to realize that such things do not belong exclusively to the medieval past: football violence, badger-baiting, bullfighting, and hideous entertainments involving animal cruelty still occur today, indicating man's timeless propensity towards violence and derivation of enjoyment from it. Medieval children were exposed to extreme violence from a young age; in a controlled, even festive, atmosphere, they were not traumatized by it but might take the opportunity it provided for play. Public executions were common and witnessed by children. In a case from 1221, Thomas of Eldersfield was condemned to hanging but, at the last moment, was shown mercy and instead was subjected to public mutilation: blinding and castration. This was carried out with gusto and relish, rather than with horror: "The eyes were thrown to the ground and the testicles used as footballs, the local lads kicking them playfully at the girls."[8] Squeamishness was not a feature of the medieval world. Cock fighting was known as the sport of the young. At one school, "on Shrove Tuesday boys had a holiday from school, and in the morning brought their fighting-cocks to their masters ... and then the boys spent their time watching the battling cocks."[9] Another favorite was cock throwing: pursuing a cock while hurling missiles at it; the stunned bird was then propped up and subjected to a further barrage until it was killed.[10]

It is interesting to note that there was a discernible level of *de haut en bas* contempt for such activities by society's higher echelons, occupied by the more refined violence of hunting. The aristocratic and literary world was frequently keen to depict the lower orders in coarse, violent terms to denote and reinforce social hierarchy. As Daniel Baraz has noted: "Differentiating and de-humanizing the non-nobles was a first step in establishing their cruelty. Bestial images of peasants were common from the twelfth century and were a topos in romance literature."[11] Jolanta Komornicka has recently added another dimension to this in highlighting the connections between peasantry, criminality, and animal imagery. Discussing the fourteenth-century French proverb "The angry villains / are half mad" ("*Villains correciez / est demi enragiés*"), she observes that "half mad" could also mean "half rabid": "*Enragiés* connoted a savage frenzy, a madness the likes of which could be found only in the uncontrolled and unreasoning violence of the rabid animal. In the proverb, then, the *villain* becomes half animal, a savage and bestial figure lurking within the shadows of human anger—a revelatory instance of the imaginative slippage between the human and the animal, especially between the lower classes and the uncontrollable beast."[12]

One might consider that the pastimes of peasant male youths, so focused on animal violence, exhibited a form of bestial reciprocity in the eyes of chivalric society, whose own youths were engaged in contrastingly disciplined, focused, and organized activity either as budding churchmen or as squires, both requiring controlled training. However, while this may represent an ideal in the literature, the involvement of schoolboys and students in games of animal violence would suggest that the reality reveals a common enjoyment of such brutal sports across the social classes. The intent of writers was to take opportunities to depict the peasantry engaging almost in "animal-on-animal" violence as they saw it, so as to dehumanize them and to justify their suppression, thereby reinforcing the social order.[13] At the same time, there may have been an element of encouraging such violent pastimes as a way for peasant youths to blow off testosterone-fueled steam.

From studies in the area of childhood and youth, especially the leading research of Nicholas Orme, it is evident that medieval boys had their equivalent of Action Man military toy figures in the form of knights and similar toys; as children grew older, toys reflected gender difference and the activities of their parents.[14] Children also used their imaginations to improvise their own toys, making horses from sticks (early hobbyhorses, one presumes) and spears from plant stems.[15] In addition to the ever-familiar pastimes of chase, swimming, and ballgames, boys' games often took military forms or had direct martial connotations: for example, in the twelfth century the game today called Conkers was called Knights.[16] Bows and arrows for boys were encouraged by adults wanting boys to play their part in what was, for most men, a military society. The Statute of Winchester of 1285 stipulated that all fifteen-year-old males should at the very minimum own a bow and arrows, expressing a predominant concern not only for army recruitment but also with the Statute's preoccupation with law and order.[17]

The crown later attempted to affect the play of young people in general with an eye to military training. Orme charts this progression from the later fourteenth century:

> In 1365 Edward III complained that people followed "dishonest and useless" games like stone casting, ball games and cock fighting, and ordered the male population to practice on feast days with bows and arrows or crossbows and bolts. The Statute of Cambridge (1388), ordered all "servants" (a term implying young men) to give up quoits, dice, stone casting and skittles, and to do archery practice on Sundays and festivals ... in 1512, a statute of Henry VIII extended the legislature to younger children ... all men with boys in their houses, aged between seven and seventeen, should provide them with a bow and two arrows, and to bring them up to shoot. Justices of the Peace were told to enforce the statute, and butts were to be set up in every town for practice on holidays.[18]

It is no coincidence, I would add, that the 1388 statute was passed at a time when the English were starting to experience setbacks in the Hundred Years War against France.

Here we see the serious aspects of boys' play, aspects that applied equally to men's pastimes. The military needs of the war led some kings to order that all existing games be replaced by archery contests: King Charles V of France prohibited dice, board games, and various ball games, "which do not serve to exercise or prepare our subjects in the use of weapons for the defense of our realm"; in Scotland in 1424, King James I "for[bade] that no man play at the fute-ball"; while in 1457, James II, with the same motive, ordered "that the fute-ball and golfe be utterly cryed down and not to be used."[19] Archery practices and competitions were commonly undertaken at the butts, which were often established in churchyards. But archery play could be very informal. One popular form of archery competition "was to shoot from a distance, even as much 200 yards, at a wooden stick fixed in a target or staked vertically in the ground, with the objective of splitting the peg with an arrow."[20] Roving was also popular; as the name implies, it involved groups roving across the countryside "shooting at random targets, sometimes to the considerable dismay of landowners."[21] As Orme claims, "These policies anticipated 19th-century ones. The Battle of Agincourt was won on the playing fields of Kenilworth, like that of Waterloo on the fields of Eton," as Wellington believed.[22] With regard to archery at least we should not be too fixated on gender: in 1503, at the age of fourteen, Henry VII's sister Margaret is recorded as having shot a buck.

Of course, violence begets violence, and aggressive play easily developed into aggressive reality. The Middle Ages had their share of disruptive anti-social elements and youth gang warfare as we have already seen. The chronicler Adam of Usk tells us how on frequent occasions in 1400, shortly after the Lancastrian usurpation of Richard II, young apprentices in London grouped themselves into gangs of Henricians or Ricardians: "The lads of the city of London, often gathering in thousands and choosing kings among themselves, made war upon each other, and fought to their utmost strength; whereby many died stricken with blows, or trampled underfoot, or crushed in narrow passages.... From such gatherings they could not be restrained, until the king wrote to their parents and masters with grievous threats to prevent them."[23]

Similarly, during the Second Barons' War (1264–1267) in England, Oxford University students sided with anti-royalist forces, being particularly antagonized when royalist forces locked the gate to their playing fields; a riot ensued and the gate was hacked down. At the battle of Northampton (1264) they fought alongside the rebel barons and "wrought great havoc against the attackers ... with slings and bows and arrows."[24] Martial play and pastimes had quickly developed into the real thing.

As we move up the social scale of sporting activity, jousting, and the world of trainee-knights was reflected in play. These could lead to serious and even fatal consequences. Court records from Yorkshire in 1219 reveal that Adam de Monceaux was killed by William Aguillon with a sword as they were playing (*ludebant*) in a friend's house.[25] In the London of 1183, William Fitz Stephen describes some of the dangerous games played by boys on the frozen Thames in London, even engaging in a form of jousting "often at the cost of cuts and broken limbs." But the boys were unconcerned about their injuries because "youth is greedy for fame and longs for victory."[26] The exposure to danger was not just part of testosterone-filled thrill seeking, but a way of preparing possible future soldiers-to-be to face mortal dangers. Fitz Stephen added that these battles on the Thames were as much preparation for real combats later as the jousts held every Sunday in Lent for the sons of rich citizens and young nobles of the royal court.

Against this background, it is but a short step to view the tournament as a serious military training ground for the aristocratic male youth. The knight would begin his training as a boy, tilting at the quintain with a lance, on foot or being pulled rapidly to a target while on a mock wooden horse. There is some popular misunderstanding of what tournaments actually constituted. Originally they were, in the very real sense, war games, involving large groups of soldiers, including infantry, ranged against each other and fighting over large tracts of countryside, like fox hunting today. These tournaments were *mêlées*. They afforded the participants the opportunity to win booty in the form of ransoms, captured armor and horses, just like in real medieval warfare. In this way, successful knights could amass fame and fortune for themselves through tourneying.[27] The most famous example of a knight as champion of the tournament circuit is William Marshal who, from humble origins, went on to become Earl of Pembroke and, in 1216, Regent of England. In one ten-month period he paired up with another combatant to capture an astonishing 103 knights at various tournaments.[28] In those times the tourney was often referred to as *hastiludium*, from which we have derived hastilude, meaning a game with spears. Single combats—or jousts—were not as popular as they were to become. Our most familiar, popular image of the tournament is actually the lists. Circa 1420, it became customary to erect a wooden barrier (or at least a rope strung above the ground with cloth draped over it), known as the tilt, down the center of the hastilude ground—the lists—to prevent the charging horses from colliding with each other. When the tilt was absent, the joust was known as "at random" or "at large." But note the lateness of this development. By this stage of development, the tournament was becoming more of an aristocratic, formalized sport and less of a training for real warfare.

Tournaments held an international appeal, with knights travelling from kingdom to kingdom to participate in the European tournament circuit. In this way, knights fought not only in their seigniorial or regional tournaments, but also in national ones. Galbert of Bruges, writing in the early twelfth century, praises Count Charles of Flanders because "he undertook chivalric exploits for the honor of his land and the training of his knights by engaging in tourneys in the lands of Normandy or France, and sometimes beyond, in this way enhancing his own fame and the power and glory of his county."[29] In England, Richard the Lionheart reversed Henry II's prohibition of tournaments—Henry feared the opportunities for unrest that they afforded—by an ordinance of 1194, which set forth that any tournaments held in England must be licensed by the king.[30]

Tournaments were therefore not merely outlets of testosterone aggression and an opportunity to gamble, show off, and make money. Important as these were, their serious purpose was training knights for war. In this they were extremely effective; indeed, they were necessary. Apart from the obvious benefits of enhancing already finely-honed riding skills and weapon-wielding in the saddle, tournaments also meant vital group practice, where knights could carry out, experiment with, and learn tactical moves as a body of men, which they could use to advantage in real combat situations, such as the famous feigned flight maneuver executed by the Normans at Hastings at 1066, and the almost unstoppable shock charge of heavy cavalry with couched lances. Furthermore, such action fostered group morale and bonding, vital elements in a successful fighting force: the combat primary group cohesion syndrome that shows men fight best for their comrades in arms over any other cause or motivation.[31] Tournaments also encouraged bravery and martial attainment for financial reward. As Matthew Bennett has noted in an important article, "these events were clearly demonstrations of masculine prowess."[32] Thus Pope Innocent II's condemnation in 1130 lambasted "these detestable markets and fairs, vulgarly called tournaments, at which knights are wont to assemble, in order to display their strength and rash boldness."[33] This desire to impress was given extra impetus when, early on in tournament development, at least from the 1130s, knights began to adopt the favors of female spectators. The early twelfth-century chronicler Geoffrey of Monmouth describes how "the knights planned a tournament and competed together on horseback, while the womenfolk watched from the top of the city walls and aroused them to passionate excitement by their flirtatious behavior."[34]

That the conditions of warfare were faithfully replicated in the training situation of a tournament can be measured by the sheer danger involved. The first known mention of a tournament is made in 1066 because it records the death of an Angevin knight, Geoffrey de Preuilly, at such an event. In 1175 in Saxony, Archbishop Wichman of Magdeburg, horrified that sixteen knights had died in tournaments over the past year, excommunicated all participants. The church, ever attempting to restrict one group of Christians from shedding the blood of another group of Christians (instead of the infidel Muslims) tried to stop tournaments in 1130 with a prohibition from Pope Innocent II in which he ordered that any knight killed in the tournament was to be refused a Christian burial.[35] Uncompromising papal disapproval could do little against the appeal of the tournament—which was, remember, a spectator sport—and in 1316 Pope John XXII revoked the prohibition.

Members of the nobility were expected to be inspiring military commanders. This was the age of the *oratores, bellatores,* and *laboratores*—those who prayed, those who fought, and those who worked—and so the nobility took leading parts in tournaments, leading to some impressive fatalities. Maurice Keen has noted that for the thirteenth century alone, illustrious victims of tournaments included: Geoffrey de Mandeville, Earl of Essex, trampled to death in 1216; Count Florence of Holland in 1223; his son Florence in 1234 and his brother William in 1238; and in 1279 Robert of Clermont, brother of King Philip III of France, "sustained in his very first tournament head injuries which left him largely incapacitated for the rest of his life."[36] In 1241 at a tournament in Nuess it is claimed that over forty knights died, many of them having seemingly been suffocated in their armor as a result of heat, dust, and exhaustion.[37] Walter of Guisborough tells us that the tournament at Chalons in 1273 quickly escalated out of control; there were so many casualties among both participants and spectators, and that so "much blood was shed" the hastilude became known "not as a tournament but is commonly called the little battle of Chalons" (*parvum bellum de Chalons*).[38] Authorities often feared aggressive male entertainments not just for the broken heads of the participants but for the opportunity they proffered for larger-scale unrest or civil insurrection. For this reason, at different times in different places, tournaments and jousting might be banned.[39]

More usually, like the requirement to practice archery, tournaments were encouraged as training for war. During Henry II's prohibitions in England, Roger of Howden describes how the king's ambitious sons travelled to France to seek tournaments because they knew that skill at war can be acquired only by practice, and that "he is not fit for battle who has never seen his own blood flow, who has not heard his teeth crunch under the blow of an opponent, or felt the full weight of his adversary upon him."[40] William of Newburgh reveals that Richard's reason for overturning his father's policy was because he saw that the French "were fiercer and better trained for war ... and he did not wish to see the French insult the knights of his kingdom as coarse and lacking skill."[41] We have seen how later tournaments were less authentic in their training of war; even by the fourteenth century the French writer Henri de Laon is lamenting the growing emollience and ceremonial nature of tournaments. Tournaments, he warned, needed to maintain their standards of toughness and ferocity, because their objective should be to identify those "who have the courage to endure bodily hardship, which is what marks out the man who is fit to lead a company ... the man who does not pause for heat or breathlessness ... To be soaked in one's own sweat and blood, that I call the true bath of honor."[42] Leaving aside Henri's personal standards of hygiene, we can appreciate the point that he is making. Writing in about 1160, the troubadour Chrétien de Troyes (author of the some of the earliest Arthurian romances), gives us this account of a tournament: "On either side the ranks tremble and a roar rises from the fight. The shock of lances is very great. Lances break and shields are riddled, the hauberks receive bumps and are torn asunder, saddles go empty and horsemen tumble, while the horses sweat and foam. Swords are quickly drawn on those who fall noisily, and some run to receive the promise of a ransom, others to stave off this disgrace."[43]

It is not surprising then, as Ralph Ferrers proclaimed in the late fourteenth century, tournaments are "where the school and study of arms is;" elsewhere they are referred to as *écoles de prouesse*.[44] From a young age most boys of the upper classes were indeed schooled in the use of arms, often informally for the lesser ranks, but rigorously for the higher ones. Training as a squire began in adolescence but could begin as young as seven, from which time a boy was expected to be able to ride well. Shulamith Shahar explains what was expected of squires: "Training was conducted in groups, and children constituted a single group (of mixed ages) within the population of the castle ... However, [unlike children in a monastery] no attempt was made to separate future knights from adult society. There were raised in the male world of sweat, weapons, stables horses, and hounds, with its ethos of courtly culture, as well as its lusts and unrestrained urges. A central role in the child's education was played by approval, and by the sanctions of group pride and shame."[45] This fostered primary group cohesion, an imperative of military training, as the youths bonded during their military apprenticeships.

This cohesion was further reinforced as the youths "also faced danger together when out hunting, which was also both an introduction to, and a substitute for, war itself."[46] Like tournaments, hunting "was a basic part of military training, for it perfected horsemanship under conditions very similar to those met on campaign. It taught boys and youths how to move in company across the countryside, instilled in them the arts of scouting and selecting a line of advance, and gave excellent training in arms, the bow against running animals and the sword and the spear against the wild boar."[47]

In Asser's *Life of King Alfred* from the early 890s, the biographer praises the future king's hunting ability as a teenager: "An enthusiastic huntsman, he strives continuously in every branch of hunting, and not in vain; for no one else could approach him in skill and success in that activity."[48] As with so much in Asser's work, the prince's boyhood years prefigured his greatness to come, most of all in defeating the Vikings and saving Wessex; Alfred's youthful hunting skills were an indication of his potential.

It is worth noting that hunting was one of the rare activities with a military emphasis that did not demarcate gender boundaries so acutely. While "hunting is traditionally considered in academic discourse in terms of the formation and reinforcement of various masculinities," Richard Almond and Amanda Richardson have both stressed the neglected role of female involvement in the sport.[49] I have already mentioned how Henry VII's sister, Margaret, killed a buck with a bow. This mixing of gender activity may partially be explained by the cultural awareness of Diana, the Roman goddess of hunting, and that the sport often became socialized and formulized as the period progressed.

The bonds youths formed during apprenticeship and hunting "were close, and often proved to be long lasting."[50] Furthermore, the "shared risk and the need to cooperate as a team helped to produce in military males the required skills, attitudes and bonds of affection that would stand them in good stead in war. It also inculcated in them a sense of shared values."[51] Jean de Bueil's fifteenth-century *Le Jouvencal* expresses this clearly: "You love your comrade so much in war. … A great sweet feeling of loyalty and of pity fills your heart on seeing your friend so valiantly exposing his body to execute and accomplish the command of our Creator. And then you are prepared to go and die or live with him, and for love not to abandon him."[52] The fourteenth-century romance of *Perceforest* is even more explicit about the long-lasting bonds formed from youth: "We have been brothers-in-arms from the very beginning, and we have been and still are bound to one another in such a way, that each will stand by the other to death if need be, saving his honor, and thus true affection has brought me to his assistance, to aid him by my body … as he would the same for me if I had need of him."[53] Keen has rightly warned that it is wrong to see such expressions as "mere chivalrous extravaganza" and that they actually reflected very real, "very close relationships."[54]

Paradoxically, all this bonding and development of the chivalric code meant that these highly trained elite warriors were reluctant to kill each other. At the battle of Bremule in 1119 Orderic Vitalis tells us that only three knights died out of nine hundred combatants because of their "fellowship in arms."[55] In the rout of the French at the battle of Lincoln in 1217, there were again only three deaths despite the one-sided nature of the engagement; Roger of Wendover attributes this solely to the close relationships between the victors and the enemy.[56] A more cynical but equally valid explanation is that a live captive was worth more than a dead one, but clearly the social networks formed had lasting and mitigating influences.

These boys with toys grew up to be men with a mission. In a darker development, many also grew up to be cheery psychopaths. The image of the troubadour as a Blondel-like figure gently strumming his lute across Europe is severely challenged by the likes of Bertrand de Born from the same era of the late twelfth century.[57] In the middle of a flowing floral praise to the pastoral delights of spring, Bertrand suddenly exclaims that the real joy of Spring lies in the new season of warfare: "I love to see tents and pavilions spread; and it gives me great joy to see, drawn up on the field, knights and horses in battle array." He continues in this blood-thirsty vein, expressing ever greater "delight," his heart being "filled with gladness" at the sight of men being struck down and at the cries of men screaming for help. Nothing gives him so much joy as "seeing at last the dead, with the pennoned stumps of lances still in their sides."[58] In the late fifteenth century, Jean de Bueil, despite having lost his father at Agincourt, echoed Bertrand de Born, declaring that "War is a joyous thing!"[59] The pleasure of play could easily develop into the pleasure of the real thing.

Sean McGlynn is Lecturer in History at Plymouth University at Strode College, Somerset.

Notes

1. Of the many works on chivalry, the standard remains Maurice Keen, *Chivalry* (New Haven, CT: Yale University Press, 1984). Also valuable are Richard Barber, *The Knight and Chivalry* (Woodbridge: Boydell Press, 1995); the five volumes in the series Christopher Harper-Bill and Ruth Harvey, eds., *The Ideals and Practice of Medieval Knighthood* (Woodbridge: Boydell Press, 1986–1992); Nigel Saul, *For Honour and Fame: Chivalry in England, 1066–1500* (London: Pimlico, 2012); and Robert Jones and Peter Coss, eds., *A Companion to Chivalry* (Woodbridge: Boydell, 2019).
2. Sean McGlynn, *By Sword and Fire: Cruelty and Atrocity in Medieval Warfare* (London: Weidenfeld and Nicolson, 2008), 1.
3. For discussions of this, see McGlynn, *By Sword and Fire*; Daniel Baraz, *Medieval Cruelty* (Ithaca: Cornell University Press, 2003); Mark Meyerson, Daniel Thiery and Oren Falk, eds., *"A Great Effusion of Blood?": Interpreting Medieval Violence* (Toronto: Toronto University Press, 2004); Richard Kaeuper, ed., *Violence in Medieval Society* (Woodbridge: Boydell, 2000); Richard Kaeuper, *Chivalry and Violence in Medieval Europe* (Oxford: Oxford University Press, 1999); Larissa Tracy, *Torture and Brutality in Medieval Literature* (Woodbridge: Brewer, 2011); Warren Brown, *Violence in Medieval Europe* (Harlow: Pearson, 2011).
4. Philippe Contamine, *War in the Middle Ages,* trans. Michael Jones (Oxford: Blackwell, 1984), xii.

5. See McGlynn, *By Sword and Fire*, 9.
6. See Antonia Gransden, "Childhood and Youth in Medieval England," *Nottingham Medieval Studies* 16 (1972): 3, for a description of a "popular ball game" with spectators in London in 1183.
7. For youth involvement in these activities, see Compton Reeves, *Pleasures and Pastimes in Medieval England* (Stroud: Alan Sutton, 1995), 100–101.
8. Robert Bartlett, *England under the Norman and Angevin Kings, 1075–1225* (Oxford: Oxford University Press, 2005), 180. See also McGlynn, *By Sword and Fire*, ch. 1.
9. Reeves, *Pleasures and Pastimes*, 100.
10. Ibid., 100–101. It is worth noting that in some literature, animals could also be regarded not merely as dumb victims of violence, undeserving of pity, but also as agents of divine and even sadistic retribution, such as the mice that gnawed to death a knight who had stolen church property. See Brown, *Violence in Medieval Europe*, 153.
11. Baraz, *Medieval Cruelty*, 125.
12. Jolanta N. Komornicka. "Man as Rabid Beast: Criminals into Animals in Late Medieval France," *French History* 28, no. 2 (2014): 157. Komornicka later notes how "Public justice shamed and degraded the individual, subordinating his person to the community and questioning his integral humanity, especially when the criminal was hanged between two dogs" (169). This, however, was not the preserve of the lower orders; see McGlynn, *By Sword and Fire*, 52.
13. See, for example, Baraz, *Medieval Cruelty*, 126.
14. Nicholas Orme, "Child's Play in Medieval England," *History Today* 51, no. 9 (2001): 50–51. This and the following paragraph draws heavily on Orme's critically acclaimed research. See also Nicholas Orme, *Medieval Children* (New Haven, CT: Yale University Press, 2001); idem, *From Childhood to Chivalry: The Education of the English Kings and Aristocracy, 1066–1530* (London: Routledge, 1984); Shulamith Shahar, *Childhood in the Middle Ages* (Routledge: London, 1992); Gransden, "Childhood and Youth in Medieval England."
15. Orme, "Child's Play," 51.
16. Conkers are horse chestnut seeds, sometimes known in the United States as "buckeyes." The game involves two opponents each holding a conker on a string. These are struck against each other, the one splintering first being the loser. This medieval game recently received recognition in North America with the inaugural North American Conker Championship of October 2012.
17. See Michael Prestwich, *Edward I* (New Haven, CT: Yale University Press, 1988), 280–281. That said, the bow also had a long association with criminality, an anonymous poet of Edward's reign complaining: "If I am a companion and know archery, my neighbour will go and say: 'This man belongs to a company' [i.e., criminal gang]" (*"Si je sei compagnoun e sache de archery / Mon veisyn irra dissant, 'cesti de compagnie'"*): Thomas Wright, *Political Songs of England, From the Reign of John to That of Edward II*, ed. Peter Coss (Cambridge: Cambridge University Press, 1839; reprinted 1996), 236.
18. Orme, *Medieval Children*, 183.
19. Cited in Trevor Dean, *Crime in Medieval Europe* (Harlow: Pearson, 2002), 55.
20. Reeves, *Pleasures and Pastimes*, 99–100.
21. Ibid., 100
22. Orme, "Child's Play," 53

23. Edward Maude Thompson, ed., *The Chronicle of Adam of Usk* (Lampeter: Llanerch, 1904, reprinted 1990), 76.
24. Harry Rothwell, ed., *The Chronicle of Walter of Guisborough* (London: Camden Society, 1957), 190.
25. Reeves, *Pleasures and Pastimes*, 96.
26. Gransden, "Childhood and Youth in Medieval England," 3.
27. For tournaments, see Richard Barber and Juliet Barker, *Tournaments* (Woodbridge: Boydell, 1989); David Crouch, *Tournament* (London: Hambledon, 2005); and Alan Murray and Karen Watts, eds., *The Medieval Tournament as Spectacle: Tourneys, Jousts and Pas d'Armes, 1100–1600* (Woodbridge: Boydell, 2020).
28. For William Marshal, see David Crouch, *William Marshal: Court, Career and Chivalry in the Angevin Empire, 1147–1219* (Harlow: Longman, 1990) and Thomas Ashbridge, *The Greatest Knight: The Remarkable Life of William Marshal* (London: Simon and Schuster, 2015).
29. Galbert of Bruges, *The Murder of Charles the Good*, ed. and trans. James Ross (Toronto: Toronto University Press, 1967), 92. I have slightly abridged the passage.
30. See John Gillingham, *Richard I* (New Haven, CT: Yale University Press, 1999), 278–279.
31. See McGlynn, *By Sword and Fire*, 247–249. On bonding, see Ruth Mazo Karras, *From Boys to Men: Formations of Masculinity in Late Medieval Europe* (Philadelphia: University of Pennsylvania Press, 2003), 20–43.
32. Matthew Bennet, "Military Masculinity in England and Northern France, c. 1050–c. 1225," in *Masculinity in Medieval Europe*, ed. Dawn Hadley (Harlow: Longman, 1999), 78.
33. Cited in Keen, *Chivalry*, 84.
34. Geoffrey of Monmouth, *The History of the Kings of England*, trans. Lewis Thorpe (Harmondsworth: Penguin, 1966), 230. For a discussion of medieval male sexuality and maturation, see Derek Neal, "Masculine Identity in Late Medieval English Society," in *Writing Medieval History*, ed. Nancy Partner (London: Bloomsbury, 2005).
35. Keen, *Chivalry*, 83–84.
36. Ibid., 87.
37. Ibid. This was a real danger in medieval knightly combats.
38. *Walter Guisborough*, 212. He describes the tournament in detail at pages 210–212.
39. Saul, *For Honour and Fame*, 35–36.
40. Roger of Howden, *Chronica*, vol. II, ed. William Stubbs (London: Rolls Series, 1869), 166–167.
41. William of Newburgh, *Historia Regum Anglicarum*, in *Chronicles of the Reigns of Stephen, Henry II and Richard I*, vol. II, ed. Richard Howlett (London: Rolls Series, 1885), 422–423.
42. Cited in Keen, *Chivalry*, 88.
43. Ibid., 85.
44. Ibid., 99.
45. Shahar, *Childhood in the Middle Ages*, 210–211. See also Matthew Bennett, "The Status of the Squire," in *The Ideals and Practices of Medieval Knighthood I*, ed. Christopher Harper-Bill and Ruth Harvey (Woodbridge: Boydell, 1987).
46. Bennett, "Military Masculinity," 73. For hunting, see Richard Almond, *Medieval Hunting* (Stroud: Alan Sutton, 2003), and Reeves, *Pleasures and Pastimes*, 103–111.

47. Frank Barlow, *William Rufus* (London: Methuen, 1980), 23.
48. Asser, *Alfred the Great*, ed. and trans. Simon Keynes and Michael Lapidge (London: Penguin, 2003), 75.
49. Almond, *Medieval Hunting*, 143–166; Amanda Richardson, "'Riding Like Alexander, Hunting Like Diana': Gendered Aspects of the Medieval Hunt and Its Landscape Settings in England and France," *Gender and History* 24, no. 2 (2012): 253–270. The quote is from Richardson, 253. My thanks to Linda Mitchell and Katherine Weikert for bringing this article to my attention, as well as the work of Naomi Sykes on medieval hunting.
50. Bennett, "Military Masculinity," 73.
51. Ibid., 73–74.
52. Cited in Johan Huizinga, *The Waning of the Middle Ages* (New York: Doubleday, 1924, reprinted 1954), 76. See also McGlynn, *By Sword and Fire*, 247–249.
53. Quoted in La Curne de Ste-Palaye, *Mémoires de l'Ancienne Chevalrie* (Paris: 1759), I:276.
54. Maurice Keen, "Brother-in-Arms," in Keen, *Nobles, Knights and Men-at-Arms in the Middle Ages* (London: Hambledon, 1996), 43.
55. Orderic Vitalis, *The Ecclesiastical History*, ed. M. Chibnall (Oxford: Oxford University Press, 1969–1981), VI:240.
56. Roger of Wendover, *The Flowers of History*, ed. Henry Hewlett (London: Rolls Series, 1887), II:219–220.
57. For troubadours, see Linda Paterson, *The World of the Troubadours: Medieval Occitan Society, c. 1100–c. 1300* (Cambridge: Cambridge University Press, 1993).
58. William Paden, Tilde Sankovith, and Patricia Stäblein, ed. and trans., *The Poems of the Troubadour Bertrand de Born* (Berkeley: University of California Press, 1986), 338–343.
59. Cited in Huizinga, *The Waning of the Middle Ages*, 76. There are now two modern critical editions of *Le Jouvencel*: Jean de Bueil, *Le Jouvencel*, ed. M. Szkilnik (Paris: Champion, 2018) and an English translation of that edition in Jean De Bueil, *Le Jouvencel*, ed. and trans. Craig Taylor and Jane H. M. Taylor (Woodbridge: Boydell, 2020).

Chapter 8

"And much more I am soryat for my good knyghts"
Fainting, Homosociality, and Elite Male Culture in Middle English Romance

Rachel E. Moss

Sir Mador went with mikel pride
Into the forest, him for to play,
That flowred was and braunched wide;
He fand a chapel in his way,
As he came by the cloughes side,
There his owne broder lay,
And there at mass he thought to abide.

A riche tomb he fand there dight
With lettres that were fair ynow;
A while he stood and redde it right;
Grete sorrow then to his herte drow;
He fand the name of the Scottish knight
The Queen Gaynor with poison slogh.
There he lost both main and might,
And over the tomb he fell in swough.[1]

In the *Stanzaic Morte Arthur*, a fourteenth-century Middle English romance, Sir Mador goes out for a pleasure ride in the forest and happens upon a tomb, thus learning of his brother's death. Pushed beyond the limits of his physical or mental ability to bear the emotional cost of this loss, he faints. Once recovered, he rides immediately to Arthur's court, demanding justice for his brother's death, and the queen is condemned to death unless a champion will fight for her. Mador, introduced 880 lines into the poem, is a plot device whose function is to put Guinevere (Gaynor) in a position where she is accused of murder. He could easily have been portrayed as a villain who falsely accuses the queen, but instead a few lines make it clear that Mador is acting on noble impulses. The poem offers only a brief description of Mador as a "hardy man and snell [swift]":[2] and so it is his reaction to his brother's death, his physical and emotional collapse in the form of a swoon, that establishes his knightly integrity and the justness of his quest for vengeance, even if the target of that quest is the wrong person.

In Middle English romances, the physical expression of male emotion serves both to reinforce norms of elite masculine behavior and to promote homosocial bonding. Mador does not faint in spite of his knightly qualities of hardiness, strength, and prowess: he faints because of them, and his swooning is literary shorthand for the nobility this fast-paced poem does not have the space to elaborate. As Barry Windeat notes, fainting occurs so frequently in medieval literature "as to pass for almost commonplace behavior"; the only unusual feature of Mador's swoon is that it takes place without witnesses, since "swoons in literature tend to be witnessed events, implicitly dramatic and performative occasions."[3]

An earlier critical impulse to view male fainting in medieval texts as effeminizing has given way to a more nuanced reading of the gendered implications of the swoon.[4] As Gretchen Mieszkowski argues, it was in the eighteenth and nineteenth centuries that fainting became specifically considered a feminine bodily act, which has colored subsequent critical readings of swooning in medieval literature.[5] Despite this work, discussion of medieval fainting remained until recently focused on heterosexual love swooning of the type seen in Chaucer's *Troilus and Criseyde*, even though fainting happens very regularly in medieval narratives and only some of the time is brought about by lovesickness.[6] Judith Weiss quite rightly argues against this narrow interpretation of the narrative function of swooning, concluding that we "must de-gender the medieval swoon," even though her analysis of French romances shows that fainting plays a key role in representations of male nobility.[7] The medieval swoon is certainly not an ungendered act. Nor is it a single type of physical response. In Windeat's terms it is a "convention-governed lexicon of medieval body language" that runs the gamut from physical concussion to a mystical dream state.[8] In the Middle Ages, fainting, which was understood to be both a medical emergency and an outward manifestation of an inward emotional or spiritual state, had multiple meanings according to the context in which it took place.[9] I argue that in Middle

English romance, when men faint in front of other men, they are providing a physical manifestation of affective, social, and political ties that together form the foundations of a homosocial society. In order to do this, I must first explain what homosociality means and why it plays a key role in upholding dominant paradigms of gendered power.

The celebration of behaviors and qualities coded as masculine, an emphasis on the value of male bonding, and the public celebration of those ties, are part of a wider cultural discourse of what we have now come to call "hegemonic masculinity."[10] As sociologist Scott Kiesling notes, an overuse of this term has resulted in a watering-down of its critical value. Rather than using "hegemonic masculinity" to represent the fluidity, contestability, and variety of masculinities of which only a particular kind is socially dominant, many researchers have begun to use it simply as a replacement for "masculinity" or "patriarchy" rather than defining it in context-specific terms.[11] R. W. Connell points out that hegemonic masculinity is "not meant to be a description of real men; rather, hegemonic masculinity represents an ideal set of prescriptive social norms."[12] Middle English romance, with its heroic archetypes, is a rich source of idealized values around medieval masculinity and masculine culture more generally.

Since the publication of Eve Sedgwick's seminal *Between Men: English Literature and Male Homosocial Desire*, the concept of male homosociality has received significant critical attention.[13] As studies in masculinities grew in prominence in the social sciences, sociological analyses of same-sex social bonding in contexts such as sports clubs and fraternities have proliferated.[14] Meanwhile, the resurgence of pop-cultural depictions of friendship between (resolutely heterosexual) men under the banner of the recently coined term "bromance" has also resulted in analysis within literary and media studies.[15] Even though scholars are happy to use "homosociality" as a shorthand term both for social bonds between persons of the same gender and for the cultural paradigm that privileges male friendship, there has been remarkably little discussion of how homosociality actually operates as a social system. It is vital that homosociality is understood not just as same-sex social relationships, but also as a cultural framework based on networks of socially codified relationships that support hegemonic norms and in so doing maintain mainstream power structures. Modern cultural discourse makes gender solidarity—in its most basic and popularly expressed form, needing "girl time" or "guy time"—seem obvious and natural, when in fact promoting and maintaining homosocial space takes time and energy.[16] Homosociality does not just manifest in a vacuum: it must be introduced, maintained, and developed in historically and geographically contingent ways.

In a patriarchal society like late medieval England, male solidarity or bonding is vital in order to maintain norms of gendered behavior and of social power. Spaces defined as homosocial attract men who want the opportunity to bond with other men, and the social interactions performed in these spaces as male bonding exercises uphold masculine values key to that particular society. Kiesling's work on modern fraternities has found that, although fraternity members might join partly to gain status or to get access to the powerful social networks into which some privileged fraternities open doors, the overriding reason men would give for joining was because they wanted access to what they saw as a desirable sociable environment populated by other young men who shared similar values and interests.[17] That is, while there were many social and political benefits to joining a fraternity, the young men who joined them were primarily motivated by personal desires for access to a shared male space.

Kiesling's analysis of the language of fraternities points to a shared vocabulary of masculine experience that problematizes the traditional reading of homosocial environments like fraternities and sports clubs as solely promoting a conventional masculinity described by Alan Klein as featuring "hypermasculine bravado and posturing, ... domination of women and other men through act and language, drinking to excess, [and] sexual conquest."[18] While other scholars have focused on the competitive nature of men's relationships with one another, Kiesling argues that the men he studies use linguistic and social strategies to create ties of solidarity and fidelity between members of a specific privileged group for their mutual benefit. In short: in homosocial spaces, friendship is an essential foundation for establishing the group's social power, a conclusion that resonated with my reading of medieval romance.

It is key that Kiesling writes about elite men, since a homosocial environment is rarely exclusive on solely gendered grounds. Modern American university fraternities tend to select members who are from similar socio-economically and racially privileged backgrounds. From monasteries to craft guilds to chivalric orders, medieval England was filled with homosocial organizations that were selective on the grounds of social status, occupation, and of course gender. Yet surprisingly, while medieval studies in recent years have seen the publication of major works on social relationships and institutions that may be described as homosocial, such as David Clark's work on male friendship and desire and Christina Fitzgerald's exploration of masculinity and guild culture, the concept of homosociality itself remains mostly uninterrogated by scholars of the Middle Ages.[19] Within medieval romance, socio-economic position, martial prowess, and cultural interests bind men either into explicitly constructed homosocial organizations such as the Round Table, or into looser but still politically significant social groups.

Malory's depiction of the formation of the Round Table shows the deliberate establishment of a homosocial environment that soon becomes attractive to elite males because it promises exclusivity, renown, and the company of other elite males. The Round Table is actually a wedding gift from Arthur's father-in-law, and Arthur says it pleases him "more than ryght grete rychesse."[20] The Table comes with 100 of its 150 seats filled—a gift with handily prepackaged excellent knights—so Arthur only has to ask Merlin to find 50 more members. He sets the bar high, asking for "knyghtes which bene of most prouesse and worship."[21] This Round Table is distinct from the court, because shortly after the Round Table is established Arthur loses eight of its knights and Pellinore notes that there are "in youre courte full noble knyghtes bothe of olde and yonge."[22] So this is an ultra-elite group within an already elite setting. Bagdemagus is a young knight who is passed over for membership, and is so upset that he goes out into the world, swearing not to return until he has earned "grete worship, and that I be worthy to be a knyght of the Round Table."[23] Individual reputation is part of the currency that gains a man entrance into this elite group, and group reputation is part of why a man wants to join in the first place. The world outside the Round Table recognizes it as the best knightly order a man can join, and Bagdemagus has to go out into that world so that the inner circle of knights will notice and acknowledge his worth. Malory repeatedly describes the Round Table as the best company of knights in the world, and when the order is irrevocably damaged by Arthur's break with Lancelot and then the dispute between Lancelot and Gawain, Arthur says "now have I loste the fayryst felyshyp of noble knyghtes that ever hylde Crystyn king."[24]

One of the great tragedies of Malory's *Morte* is that the breaking of the Round Table means that war can no longer be, in Geraldine Heng's terms, a "fusion to a corps of knights whose individual egos, boundaries and identities are temporarily dissolved in the affective intensity of a glorious common purpose."[25] In romance, the battlefield should be the ideal homosocial space, where individuality is sublimated into a collective elite identity. The *Alliterative Morte Arthur*, with its close attention to both the strategic details and the psychological consequences of battle, provides many good examples, such as this one:

> Then our chevalrous men changen their horses,
> Chases and choppes down cheftaines noble,
> Hittes full hertely on helmes and sheldes,
> Hurtes and hewes dow hethen knightes!
> Kettle-hattes they cleve even to the shoulders;
> Was never such a clamour of capitaines in erthe![26]

The repetition of *ch* and *h* sounds in this extract not only propels the action forward; it also gives the sense of a great mass of men acting as one body, moving tirelessly onward through the ranks of the enemy. This homosocial space offers a physical and emotional unity rarely replicated elsewhere, because it offers "a group communion of authorized violence."[27]

War allows knights to fulfill their primary function as mounted warriors and it is a place that provides opportunities for demonstrations of collective masculinity, both in terms of physical endeavor and also in the expression of homosocial bonds. Naturally, then, when the affective bonds between men in romance have been considered it has mostly been in the context of the battlefield. But these ties do not spring up fully formed in wartime; part of the reason that knights are able to become a unified body in battle is because their social and affective bonds have been well established in advance. Indeed, in order for the homosocial group to be established and validated, it may at times need the presence of outsiders to reinforce the value of its actions. A good example of this is in the clearly gendered space of the tournament, where women are key as witnesses to the action, but that action is exclusively male. In *Bevis of Hampton,* the hero wins a tournament *and* the heart of a princess, who witnesses his prowess:

> So Beves demeinede him that dai,
> The maide hit in the tour say.
> Hire hertte gan to him acorde,
> That she wolde have him to lorde[28]

Yet although the tournament is officially established to find the princess a husband, the reason Bevis and his companion Terri have entered is because, in Terri's words, "We scholle lete for non nede, / That we ne scholle manliche forth us bede!"[29] That is, he is concerned that their manly virtue or valor should not be called into question, rather than because either of them state a desire to win a bride. That their performance is primarily for their peers is implied by the text's emphasis on their admiration by "barouns of renoun."[30] The functions of the tournament are simultaneously homosocial and heteronormative, and allow Terri and Bevis to demonstrate their rightful place amongst their peer group, as well as their worth as prospective suitors.

Bevis and Terri have a strong friendship bond that by this point in the narrative is well established. The reader is introduced to Terri a couple of thousand lines earlier, where he is sent by his father Saber to see if he can find out what happened to Bevis. Saber, Bevis's former teacher, has been troubled since Bevis was sold to Saracens by the hero's wicked mother. Terri meets Bevis, but does not recognize him, and Bevis tells him that the lost child was killed by Saracens.

> Terri fel ther doun and swough [swooned],
> His her, his clothes he al to-drough.
> Whan he awok and speke mighte,
> Sore a wep and sore sighte
> And seide: "Allas, that he was boren!
> Is me lord Beves forloren!"[31]

The function of this scene is twofold: to show Bevis that Terri can be trusted, and to show the reader that Terri—to whom they have been introduced only a handful of lines previously—is noble-hearted, his emotional response to the thought of Bevis's death demonstrating that he is a suitable companion for the hero. This function of the swoon is well established in medieval romance, as Judith Weiss points out about the French romance *Gui de Warewic.* As she notes, it is men who do the fainting in this romance, because "it is compassion or *pité* which Gui and Terri feel, that sign of true nobility," which causes Terri to swoon on recognizing Gui.[32] Writing about romantic love,

Mieszkowski notes that the capacity for "extraordinarily intense, idealizing love is an attribute of greatness in these romances, and fainting is a sign of that capacity."[33] This seems even more accurate when recording the reaction of men to the loss of beloved comrades. In the *Alliterative Morte,* the king swoons and weeps over Gawain's corpse, cradling his nephew's body and mourning so heartily that if had not been interrupted by Sir Ewain, "His bold herte had bristen for bale at that stounde."[34] It is partly because of the great loss of Gawain that Arthur's grief is so intense, but it is also because he has such manly feelings.

Given a happier ending than Gawain, Terri's loyalty to Bevis is rewarded by him being married to a princess. This raises him to the rank he has earned by his innate good qualities, the first of which is his devotion to his lord. Terri has the capacity for a kind of heroic empathy that is expressed in physical form by fainting and weeping. Like Sir Mador in the *Stanzaic Morte Arthur,* the swoon here is shorthand, allowing us in only a few lines to understand the virtuous qualities within a character with whom we have previously had a very limited acquaintance. Once again, a short stanza about fainting stands in for a rich cultural discourse about nobility and male virtue.

The faint in *Bevis of Hampton* also has the function of in one stroke reaffirming the affective ties that bound Terri and Bevis when they were children, and of transforming them into a suitably adult bond between men. Swooning is useful to both affirm and create bonds between men; it can be a way of marking and strengthening an existing relationship, or allowing an entry-point into forming a meaningful relationship between two men. This kind of swooning typically happens at a point in the narrative where there has been a combination of physical endeavor and a period of heightened emotions: a crisis point brings to the surface the overwhelmingly strong nature of a particular male bond, leading to the swoon.

In *Sir Degaré,* the crisis point is a revelation. In this romance, the foundling Degaré has been searching for his father for a long time and across many miles when he comes across an unknown knight who accuses him of trespass. A fiercely physical fight between the two commences:

> Togider thai riden with gret raundoun,
> And aither bar other adoun.
> With dintes that thai smiten there,
> Here stede rigges toborsten were.[35]

The men are too evenly matched, and so are unable to defeat each other; but they do push themselves to the brink of exhaustion. Thus, when Degaré draws the broken sword and is recognized by his father, both men swoon, presumably from the intensity of the realization coupled with the great physical strain they have just borne:

> "O Degarre, sone mine!
> Certes ich am fader thine!

> And bi thi swerd I knowe hit here:
> The point is in min aumenere."
> He tok the point and set therto;
> Degarre fel iswone tho,
> And his fader, sikerli,
> Also he gan swony.[36]

This scene has a far greater emotional and physical intensity than Degaré's romantic scenes. *This* is the climactic moment of the romance, far more than Degaré's brief love affair, and it is one that allows for an outpouring of all Degaré's hopes and resentments. Degaré swoons because he is overwhelmed, as he has finally found the father for whom he has been searching all his adult life, and also because he is guilt-ridden, knowing he could have killed his father: "The sone cride merci there / His owen fader of his misdede."[37] The fairy knight's reason for fainting is not as clearly stated, but given he also swoons at the moment of revelation, it seems likely that his feelings mirror Degaré's: finally he has his son, and he recognizes that he could have killed that son in a petty squabble over boundaries. Despite the fact that they have just come from an episode of great antagonism and a real physical fight that put them both at risk of death, their mutual, simultaneous fainting shows a moment of perfectly realized harmony in their feelings. If the point of Degaré's sword being fitted to his father's blade were not enough to prove their relationship, their mutual swoon proves it beyond doubt. They are, for a moment, in emotional accord powerful enough to make them pass out.

Similar moments of shared emotional crisis are seen between men who have received bad news about a third party. In Malory's *Morte*, Arthur and Gawain both swoon together because Lancelot has killed Gaheris and Gareth in his desperate rescue attempt of Guinevere. Arthur has already heard this news and swooned over it, and then Gawain arrives, is told the news and faints, and then goes to his uncle and they swoon together.

> "A, myne uncle kynge Arthure! My good brothir sir Gareth ys slayne, and so ys mi brothir sir Gaherys, whych were two noble knyghts." Than the kyng wepte and he bothe, and so they felle on sownynge.[38]

To the modern reader this might sound almost farcical, but there is certainly no sense in the text that this is in any way funny. Modern sensibilities about appropriate male behavior result in expectations that men will "buck each other up" in times of crisis. In medieval romance, such a response to a tragedy of this scale would be inconceivable. While I have found nothing in Middle English that matches the scale of twenty thousand men collectively swooning over the death of Roland, the "sympathetic faint" has an established place in Middle English literature.[39] In *Sir Amadace*, for instance, "Thenne all the mene in that halle, / Doune on squonyng [swooning] ther con thay falle" when their lord is faced with the horrific choice between breaking a solemn vow and killing his wife and child.[40] With a similar empathetic understanding, rather than consoling one another, Malory's Arthur and Gawain weep and faint together. Seeing each other's grief reminds them of their own, mirroring and magnifying it so that the only appropriate emotional response is to pass out. In this context, a problem shared is not a problem halved; a hero's sorrow is ideally expressed to the full through the mechanism of sharing it with someone who understands his grief. Anything less would not be a fitting tribute to those he has lost.

Gawain weeps because he has lost his brothers, but also because they have been killed by Lancelot, who "my good brother sir Gareth ... loved ... more than me and all my kynne," the man who made Gareth a knight: a relationship that in Malory's work in particular and in romance generally often forms an extremely strong bond between men. In Gawain's mind, his brother has not only been murdered, but also betrayed. Arthur weeps because he has lost two excellent knights, because he has anticipated Gawain's grief and feels keenly for him, and because he feels the negative impact on his fellowship:

> wyte you well, my harte was never so hevy as hit ys now. And much more I am soryat for my good knyghtes losse than for the losse of my fayre quene; for quenys I myght have inow, but such a felysship of good knyghtes shall never be togydirs.[41]

Arthur has foresight enough to know that this is the end of the Round Table. His swoon marks not only the death of two of his nephews and his surviving nephew's grief, but also the coming break-up of a network of men. Arthur is not experiencing a pragmatic upset at the political disruption the end of the Round Table will cause; he feels a deeply personal anguish at the loss of the fellowship of men who are much more significant in his life than any wife can be.

However, this is not just a moment of shared pain. While that would be valuable in the narrative in itself, it has a further function: that of reiterating a shared bond. At the moment when the Round Table is most in crisis, Arthur and Gawain turn to one another and reaffirm their familial and courtly bond; Gawain calls him "myne uncle kyng Arthure,"[42] juxtaposing their two relationships: as family members and as lord and retainer. Their shared moment of fainting and weeping is psychologically reassuring, because at a time when both men feel betrayed, for different reasons, by Lancelot, they are comforted by the persistence of their bonds with one another.

This is also significant when we consider where fainting happens. Some fainting does happen in private, which seems to be particularly common when fainting is induced by romantic feelings. Chaucer's Troilus, for instance, famously swoons in Criseyde's chamber. When swooning is induced because of a man's feelings for another man, however, he is much more likely to do it in company. Key to the swoon is that it is witnessed by the homosocial group to which the swooner belongs. In this episode between Gawain and Arthur, we are at Arthur's court. Arthur is brought the news and faints;

the text does not specify a location, but on awakening Arthur addresses his "fayre felowis," and "some knyghtes" reply.[43] This is not swooning in a private chamber; Arthur is here fainting, if not in front of the whole court, at least in front of a number of the elite members of that court. It is important that on waking he refers to the witnesses as "fellows," which reminds them that they are companions and comrades, and suggests he thinks they will have an empathetic understanding of his grief. There is no indication that he changes location upon Gawain's arrival and their mutual swoon, and so the significance of Arthur's faint is reinforced through repetition in front of the same audience. Here the swoon is translated and thus given additional meaning by the homosocial peer group. The swoon is not read in isolation but is incorporated into the witnesses' understanding of the reputation of the swooner, the relationship that is understood between swooner and object-of-swoon (or mutual swooners in the case of a double faint), and the reputation of the swoon-object. The more highly each of these elements is valued by witnesses, the more significant the impact of the swoon.

What happens between Arthur and Gawain is given depth and complexity because it is performed in front of witnesses. Performativity does not negate the sincerity of their emotions; Gawain and Arthur feel as keenly about the death of Gareth and Gaheris as the weeping and swooning Arthur in the *Alliterative Morte* does over the death of Gawain when he declares: "This real red blood run upon erthe! / It were worthy to be shrede and shrined in gold,"[44] which turns Gawain's blood into a relic and thus his nephew into a saint. Malory's Arthur is in his court, and must as a monarch perform his expected role, as must Gawain as one of his most celebrated knights. Their mutual swooning and mourning reinforces, in the mind of a group that has been shaken by the loss of Lancelot to exile and also the knights Lancelot killed, that they are still bonded together. Although Arthur recognizes that the Round Table can never be whole again, by sharing his nephew's grief he demonstrates to his court that he is still emotionally invested in their remaining fellowship. It is both a profoundly human moment that demonstrates the personal nature of the lord/retainer bond, and also a perfectly political moment of social bonding that reminds the witnesses that they are led by extraordinary men, capable of extraordinarily heroic feeling.

In his study of American fraternities, Kiesling reported on a speech intended to boost flagging membership that was given by a young man to his former fraternity. He earnestly reinforced the value to the individual of feeling like a member of a homosocial collective: "I was wearin' my letters, I felt safe, I felt comfortable y'know, and hey I'm Gamma Chi Phi here I'm surrounded by all these people, I feel OK, those were the best feelings *ever*."[45] For Malory's Arthur, the stakes are much higher than a dwindling population of a fraternity house. He is faced with the loss of the greatest community of knights that the world has known. He already knows that the perfect homosocial unit of the Round Table cannot be saved, but he must be king to those who remain. In his act of fainting, he grieves for a world that is lost, but he also reminds his audience of what is truly valuable to men like them: individual heroism and capacity for great feeling, and the collective ability to form lasting bonds that, because of their social and political value, are more important than ties of blood or marriage. Men in romance do not just faint because they have lost; they faint because they love, and their swooning is both a commemoration of grief and a celebration of masculine bonds.

Rachel E. Moss is Lecturer in History at the University of Northampton.

Notes

1. *Stanzaic Morte Arthure*, ll. 888–903, in *King Arthur's Death: The Middle English Stanzaic Morte Arthur and Alliterative Morte Arthure,* ed. Larry D. Benson (Kalamazoo, MI: Medieval Institute Publications, 1994). Summary: Sir Mador went into the forest for recreation. He came across a tomb at a chapel, and the inscription revealed the name of his brother, murdered by Queen Gaynor (Guinevere). On reading this, he swooned over the tomb.
2. *SMA*, 884.
3. Barry Windeat, "The Art of Swooning in Middle English," in *Medieval Latin and Middle English Literature: Essays in Honour of Jill Mann,* ed. Christopher Cannon and Maura Nolan (Cambridge: D. S. Brewer, 2011), 211–212.
4. Chaucer's Troilus has been a particular focus of criticism that sees fainting as emasculating and feminising, as his swoon in Criseyde's chamber has been characterised as evidence of his passivity as a lover. Jill Mann and Gretchen Mieszkowski have offered robust criticism of this: Jill Mann, "Troilus' Swoon," *Chaucer Review 15, no.* 4 (1980): 319–335, and Gretchen Mieszkowski, "Revisiting Troilus's Faint," in *Men and Masculinities in Chaucer's Troilus and Criseyde,* ed. Tison Pugh and Marcia Smith Marzec (Cambridge: D. S. Brewer, 2008), 43–57. See also Windeat, "The Art of Swooning," and Judith Weiss, "Modern and Medieval Views on Swooning: The Literary and Medical Contexts of Fainting in Romance," in *Medieval Romance, Medieval Contexts,* ed. Michael Staveley Cicho and Rhiannon Purdie (Cambridge: D. S. Brewer, 2011), 121–134.
5. Mieszkowski, "Revisiting Troilus's Faint," 45–47. See also Judith Weiss on Mieszkowski's work in "Modern and Medieval Views on Swooning," 121–122.
6. Troilus's swoon takes place at II. 1086–1092. *Troilus and Criseyde*, in *The Riverside Chaucer,* ed. Larry D. Benson, 3rd ed. (Oxford: Oxford University Press, 1987). See Windeat's "The Art of Swooning" for a clear overview of the multiple contexts in which swooning occurs in medieval narratives.
7. Weiss, "Modern and Medieval Views on Swooning," 122. For her discussion of noble male swooning, see the same article, 128, which I discuss further later in this essay.
8. Windeat, "The Art of Swooning," 212, 225.
9. Ibid., 225. On the medieval medical understanding of swooning, see Elizabeth M. Liggins, "The Lovers' Swoons in *Troilus and Criseyde,*" *Parergon* 3, no. 1 (1985): 96.

10. The most commonly cited discussion of hegemonic masculinity is R. W. Connell's *Gender and Power: Society, the Person and Sexual Politics* (Sydney, Australia: Allen & Unwin, 1987). For the historiography of the field since then, see R. W. Connell and James W. Messerschmidt, "Hegemonic Masculinity: Rethinking the Concept," *Gender and Society* 19, no. 6 (2005): 829–859.
11. Scott Fabius Kiesling, "Homosocial Desire in Men's Talk: Balancing and Re-Creating Cultural Discourses of Masculinity," *Language in Society* 34, no. 5 (2005): 701.
12. R. W. Connell, *Masculinities* (Cambridge: Polity Press, 1995), 76. Steven L. Arxer provides further historiographical context for this in "Hybrid Masculine Power: Reconceptualizing the Relationship between Homosociality and Hegemonic Masculinity," *Humanity & Society* 35, no. 4 (2011): 392–393.
13. Eve Kosofsky Sedgwick, *Between Men: English Literature and Male Homosocial Desire* (New York: Columbia University Press, 1985).
14. Some recent examples I have found useful include Alan Klein, "Dueling Machos: Masculinity and Sport in Mexican Baseball," and Laurence de Garis, "'Be a buddy to your buddy': Male Identity, Aggression, and Intimacy in a Boxing Gym," both in *Masculinities, Gender Relations, and Sport*, ed. Jim McKay, Michael A Messner, and Donald Sabo (Thousand Oaks, CA: Sage, 2000), 67–86 and 87–107, and the collection *Men's Health and Illness: Gender, Power and the Body*, ed. Michael S. Kimmel and Michael A. Messner (Boston, MA: Allyn and Bacon, 1995).
15. See Amanda Lott's discussion of the word "bromance" in a media context in her *Cable Guys: Television and Masculinities in the 21st Century* (New York: New York University Press, 2014), 8. Chapters 4 and 5 extensively deal with male friendship in cable media. See also the collection *Reading the Bromance: Homosocial Relationships in Film and Television*, ed. Michael DeAngelis (Detroit, MI: Wayne State University Press, 2014).
16. Many modern depictions of same sex friendship are built around the idea that having friends of the same gender is a vital part of a happy life. For example, in the recent film *I Love You, Man*, the hero is happily engaged to a woman and has several close friends, all of whom are female. The story is focused on his search for a best man for his wedding, and the underlying message of the film is that the hero's life has been lacking the crucial element of male friendship. *I Love You, Man*, dir. John Hamburg (De Line Pictures, 2009). See also analysis by Peter Forster, "Rad Bromance (or *I Love You, Man*, But We Won't Be Humping on Humpday)," in DeAngelis, *Reading the Bromance*, 191–212.
17. Kiesling, "Homosocial Desire in Men's Talk," 705–706.
18. Klein, "Dueling Machos," 68.
19. David Clark, *Between Medieval Men: Male Friendship and Desire in Early Medieval English Literature* (Oxford: Oxford University Press, 2009); Christina M. Fitzgerald, *The Drama of Masculinity and Medieval English Guild Culture* (Basingstoke, Hampshire: Palgrave Macmillan, 2007).
20. Thomas Malory, *Malory: Works*, ed. Eugène Vinaver, 2nd ed. (Oxford: Oxford University Press, 1971), 60.
21. Ibid., 60.
22. Ibid., 80.
23. Ibid., 81.
24. Ibid., 685.

25. Geraldine Heng, *Empire of Magic: Medieval Romance and the Politics of Cultural Fantasy* (New York: Columbia University Press, 2003), 176.
26. Summary: Our chivalrous men changed their horses, chopped down noble chieftains, hewed down heathen knights: there was never such a clamour of captains. *Alliterative Morte Arthure,* in *King Arthur's Death,* ed. Benson, ll. 2989–2994.
27. Heng, *Empire of Magic,* 176.
28. Summary: because of the way Bevis behaved that day, the maiden's heart began to desire him as her lord. *Bevis of Hampton,* ll. 3827–3830, in *Four Romances of England,* ed. Ronald B. Herzman, Graham Drake, and Eve Salisbury (Kalamazoo, MI: Medieval Institute Publications, 1999).
29. *Bevis,* ll. 3777–3778.
30. *Bevis* l. 3791.
31. Summary: Terri swooned, and tore his hair and clothing. When he awoke he wept for the loss of his lord Bevis. *Bevis,* ll. 1309–1314.
32. Weiss, "Modern and Medieval Views on Swooning," 128.
33. Mieszkowski, "Revisiting Troilus's Faint," 50.
34. Summary: his bold heart would have burst from sorrow. *Alliterative Morte,* l. 3974
35. Summary: they fought fiercely, unable to bring each other down. They struck such powerful blows that their horses' backs were broken. *Sir Degaré,* in *The Middle English Breton Lays,* eds. Anne Laskaya and Eve Salisbury (Kalamazoo, MI: Medieval Institute Publications, 1995), ll. 1042–1045.
36. Summary: the fairy knight says he is Degaré's father; he recognises the sword, and has the matching point in his pouch. When they put the sword pieces together, both men faint. *Degaré,* ll. 1058–1065.
37. *Degaré,* ll. 1066–1067.
38. Malory, 686.
39. This mass swooning occurs shortly after the death of the hero. Gerald J. Brault, ed., *The Song of Roland,* 2 vols. (University Park: Pennsylvania State Press, 1978), vol. 2, ll. 2415–2416.
40. *Sir Amadace,* in *Amis and Amiloun, Robert of Cisyle, and Sir Amadace,* ed. Edward E. Foster (Kalamazoo, MI: Medieval Institute Publications, 1997), ll. 786–787.
41. Summary: Arthur says he grieves more for the loss of his knights than for his queen, because he might easily have other queens, but there shall never be another such fellowship of knights. Malory, 685.
42. Ibid., 686.
43. Ibid., 685.
44. *Alliterative Morte,* ll. 3990–3991,
45. Kiesling, "Homosocial Desire in Men's Talk," 709.

Chapter 9

Wrist Clasps and Patriliny
A Hypothesis

Frank Battaglia

"Dress and jewellery [sic] played a major part in constituting individual and group identity in early Anglo-Saxon England," archaeologists continue to remind us, with women's roles being pivotal in the establishment of "sixth-century kindred relationships and status."[1] Such observations are a consequence of our information about social groupings in early England being largely derived from analysis of funerary remains, with visible or "even ... ostentatio[us] ... furnished burial" regarded as "the defining characteristic of the 'Early' Anglo-Saxon period."[2] Thus, whether by brooches, wrist clasps or other equipment, "the identification of ethnic groups in the [early] Anglo-Saxon period relied almost entirely on female-associated items."[3]

However, Sam Lucy recently expressed some surprise that, over the past one hundred years, this fact "does not appear to have struck many [scholars] as odd."[4] I, too, have found the attribution surprising, and offer this hypothesis to explain it: in early Anglo-Saxon ethnicities, older matrilineal tribal identities—that is, social networks based on female kinship–were being displaced as newer patrilineal structures were consolidated. The premise parallels Tania Dickinson's in pondering that the designs of Anglo-Saxon saucer brooches worn by women derived from prestige male dress ornament. "This phenomenon may indicate paradoxically," she said, "that kin-groups were dominated by men, whose status was communicated vicariously through the ornamenting of their womenfolk."[5]

The acknowledgement of women in emerging "leading kindred" would, surprisingly, help enact the abandonment of matriliny in the Anglo-Saxon social fabric. Recognition was accorded to women who had formed patrilineal unions—at that point, I suggest, still an emerging family structure—with higher status males. Nonetheless, this consideration of elite women might have masked an abjection of the authority of women known earlier in Germanic tribes.

Significantly, wrist clasp use had a southern limit that corresponds to a later political boundary, so I will focus on this Anglian phenomenon. Tracing the origin of these female accessories will bring us to Scandinavia and an unexpected connection with the *Beowulf* poem, including two consistently mistranslated passages about patriliny. The Anglian experience involved a course correction away from matrilineal traditions among both Germanic and British populations, so, along with some fairly clear evidence from Roman-period British and lower Rhine inscriptions, a sketch of the background of matriliny in northern Europe will be offered. Social formations of the first millennium CE apparently representing female systems of ancestry may be seen to have their origins much earlier, before the Iron Age and the Bronze Age, in the Neolithic Period when horticulture and the raising of food animals became bases of subsistence.[6]

Matriliny in Europe from the Neolithic

The earliest crop-raising cultures of northern Europe had been matrilineal, and traditions and social organizations of that derivation survived in some areas into historical time. H. M. Chadwick offered this view of Germanic,[7] Irish,[8] Celtic, Roman, Greek,[9] as well as Pictish peoples,[10] and Colin Renfrew has argued that the broch people of northern Britain, whose last days included a probable treaty accommodation with the Romans, preserved a social structure established in the Neolithic.[11] My own work on the Picts offered a diagnostic for discerning matriliny in the distribution of residences, and reached similar conclusions about the Picts' descent from the era that originated agriculture, animal husbandry, and the making of pottery.[12]

The earliest fully Neolithic culture of Northern Europe and south Scandinavia was the Funnel Beaker Culture. A recent analysis concluded that consistency of ceramic design over fifteen generations at Skogsmossen, Västmanland, Sweden must indicate female communities of practice and a social system based on matrilineal descent.[13] I have proposed that Scandinavian place-names preserving memory of cult rituals honoring the Germanic collective female deities, the *dísir*, derive from religious practices of the Funnel Beaker Culture, with the place-name *Disavin*, for example, originally being attached to the Alvastra Pile dwelling, a site that has been investigated archaeologically for one hundred years.[14]

Honoring of wrist clasp-wearing females will be suggested below to have mediated a general abjection of Germanic women's authority. In one indication of that former authority, D. H. Green found "the most telling evidence" of a religious dimension to the "legal practices [of the] Germanic assembly" in second-century inscriptions which seem to derive the legitimacy, let alone the very names of various kinds of *thing* from "helping goddesses."[15] Swedish assemblies in the name of the *dísir* would be conducted until the thirteenth century.[16] A large body of epigraphy recording devotion to ancestral female deities, comprising more than 645 examples, from the lower Rhine of the second and third centuries, with a few from Hadrian's Wall and other areas of Britain, seems to indicate exactly that Germanic tribal identity had earlier been constituted through females, an inference supported in numerous studies.[17]

Matriliny may be discerned in the distribution of settlements within a landscape because, among matrilineal peoples, both males and females continue to have functions in the family of origin. A clustering of residences is therefore common, rather than the dispersal of households more familiar among families organized patrilineally.[18] The so-called Celtic field systems of northern Europe are a fossilized landscape where these patterns may be read.[19] The principle is manifest in the remains of many British farms from the Roman period. J. T. Smith in *Roman Villas, A Study in Social Structure* found a number of cases, especially in Britain, where a villa structure seemed to incorporate two separate social entities.[20] Dramatically illustrating the phenomenon is the Gloucestershire villa Marshfield-Ironmonger's Piece (Figure 9.1). Here round houses, which had been clustered together on either side of a boundary wall, were later combined into a villa built across the boundary and

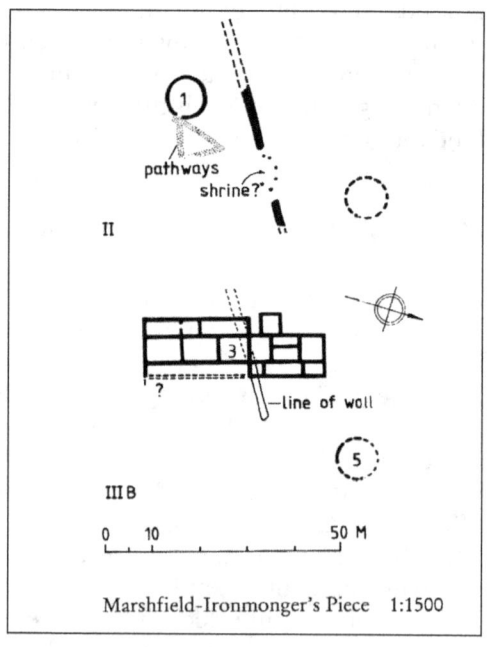

Figure 9.1 Two stages in the development of a Gloucestershire Roman villa: with Phase II depicting an approximately first century CE structure and Phase III B probably built in the late third century. *Source:* Smith, *Roman Villas*, figure 66.

"comprising two ... houses built end to end and [, remarkably,] facing opposite ways."[21] Some, at least, of these villas incorporating separate social entities apparently involved exogamous subgroups of a matrilineal British tribe that were able to intermarry.[22]

However, by the early Anglo-Saxon period, matrilineal traditions both of Britain and of Germanic Europe were being set aside in favor of the patrilineal Anglian tribal structure.

Construction of Anglo-Saxon Funerary Traditions

Funerary rituals in which the deceased was accompanied with metal grave goods have been understood to characterize the early Anglo-Saxon period, but the time span over which that was true has now narrowed. According to Christopher Scull, "[t]he suite of female dress accessories conventionally considered typically Anglo-Saxon, and the ... furnished burial tradition of which they were a part, now appear to be a feature of the later fifth and the first half of the sixth centuries,"[23] approximately the period during which wrist clasps formed part of high status Anglian women's dress. Scull has emphasized that previous Anglo-Saxon furnished inhumations expressed a militaristic elite's notions of Insular provincial culture and late Imperial identity. However, distinctive in burial rites after about 475 CE were material culture suites clearly derived from Northern Germanic antecedents of the earlier fifth century.[24] Claims of Scandinavian origin in a group descended from a warrior god formed a cultural package with these material suites and expressed a new political mentality.[25]

In the last quarter of the fifth century funerary accessories would become starkly *dichotomous* gendered assemblages.[26] That is, datable artifacts found with bodies identifiable skeletally as males, when this can be determined, were virtually never the same as those with bodies identifiable as females. Male "standard kits" had weapons, whereas in funerary rites for females, jewelry and beads focused attention more on their own bodies.[27] The gender differentiation would be so severe that the 2013 comprehensive *Chronological Framework* for sixth- and seventh-century burials had to create separate sequences for male and female grave goods.[28] According to Nick Stoodley, "[m]ortuary ritual provided a medium for the symbolic expression of clearly defined gender boundaries."[29]

Before about 475, however, materials with various gender or religious implications formed part of Anglo-Saxon funerary practice. The middle years of the cemetery at Spong Hill, Norfolk, for example, saw upticks in several kinds of ritual observance disproportionally greater than any increase in numbers using the site. Among some 2,300 human burials, a horse was cremated as a companion animal on a pyre at least 214 times. This ceremony was carried out for women as well as men during the entire 130-year span of Spong Hill's use as a cemetery (Table 9.1). During phase B, ending about 480 CE, it was practiced in comparable numbers for men and women.[30]

Table 9.1 Horse cremations at Spong Hill accompanying humans whose biological sex could be determined

	Number of horse cremations	% of male cremations with horses	% of female cremations with horses
Phase A	39	10.4%	4.4%
Phase A/B	38	14.8%	3.4%
Phase B	89	11.4%	9.4%
Phase B/C	6	17% of small sample	17% of small sample
Phase C	11	Sample of sexed cremations too small	

A different tradition, the use of ground burnt possibly *human* bone as a pottery temper, is also represented at Spong Hill. The custom had been attested between 175 and 325 CE on the Danish island Funen adjacent to the Angeln homeland in north Germany. The practice derived from matrilineal Germanic religious traditions probably related to the veneration of the *dísir*, but distorted and reinscribed as Grendel's cannibalism and his mother's monstrosity in *Beowulf*.[31] A small number of cinerary urns were being tempered with bone at the inception of Spong Hill; the number increased in Phase A/B even though fewer cremations date from that period, and declined in Phase B when one such ceramic, however, was stamp-linked with a family group in another Norfolk cemetery (Table 9.2).[32] "Community identities," Mary Chester-Kadwell has generalized, "were not fixed in the fifth century, but were constantly changing as belief and practice were renegotiated generation by generation."[33]

It must be mentioned that "a third to a half of [the] burials in … early Anglo-Saxon cemeteries"[34] were not given the metal-furnished funerary rites said to characterize the fifth and sixth centuries. These other deceased were buried either with no goods at all or with accessories like a belt buckle that might be found with either male or female skeletons. Were they slaves? Subject persons? Native Britons? Or did survivors simply not choose to mark them in death with items from the standard kit? Although these have been matters of debate, radiocarbon dating is making clear that "unfurnished or very sparsely furnished inhumation was typical of post-Roman British communities in the fifth century," and continued to be in western Britain and Wales.[35] Conversely, how many furnished graves represent native British females or males who had chosen, or whose survivors had chosen, to declare with their death ritual an affiliation with the Germanic immigrants?[36]

Table 9.2 Spong Hill ceramics with bone-ash temper

Phase[a]	Cremations with bone-ash temper urns	Other ceramics	Burial group[b]	Stamp group	Style group
A 400/420 to 450 CE	1684		66		
	3295				
Phase A/B	1429				
	2086				
	2310				
	2606		183		
	2652		200		79 (with one other)[c]
	2775		217		
	2887				
	3234		(with 3230)		
Phase B c. 450 to 470/490 CE	1488				
	1955				
	2292		155	44 (with two Spong others)[d]	
	2323				14 (with nine others)
	3292			47 (with five others)	
	Two other cremations[e]				
Phase C		Shards from settlement buildings[f]			
Unphased		Shards with cremation urns in settlement pit 2341[g]			

[a] "Accepted phase," incorporating all factors, Catherine Hills and Sam Lucy, *Spong Hill Part IX: Chronology and Synthesis* (Cambridge: McDonald Institute, 2013), Appendix 5, 365–407.
[b] A Burial Group is thought to represent a "family burial plot," Hills and Lucy, *Spong Hill*, 162.
[c] Hills and Lucy, *Spong Hill*, Table 3.2, "Style groups," 167.
[d] Hills and Lucy, *Spong Hill*, Table 3.1, "Stamp groups," 364. Caistor-by-Norwich (Nfk) cremation W30 also belongs to this Stamp Group: 321.
[e] Cremation identifications are not provided in Table 3.12, Hills and Lucy, *Spong Hill*, 222, which, for Fabric 10, gives the frequency for Phases as: "A, 1; A/B, 9; B, 6; C cremations, 0; C inhumations, 0; unassigned to Phase, 1; Total 17." Following Appendix 5, 377 and 402, the current table places both 1684 and 3295 in Phase A.
[f] Stuart Friedenson, Vera Friedenson, and Robert Rickett, "Early Saxon Pottery from Settlement Contexts," in *The Anglo-Saxon Cemetery at Spong Hill, North Elmham, Part VII: The Iron Age, Roman and Early Saxon Settlement*, East Anglian Archaeology 73, ed. Robert Rickett (Dereham: Norfolk Museums Service, 1995), 126.
[g] Cremation urns 2518, 2352, and part of 2345, all without bone-ash temper: Friedenson, Friedenson, and Rickett, "Early Saxon," 55.

Female Anglian Identity

A particular costume came to identify a fifth- or sixth-century woman of Britain as Anglian (Figure 9.2).[37] Her tubular gown could be augmented by a brooch, or pair of brooches, in slightly differing positions, and beads. Use of a possibly third, central brooch was a distinctive feature of Anglian dress, as were "girdle hangers" and a pair of metal sleeve fasteners—a kind of female cuff-link—called wrist clasps.[38] They formed a key element of an influential argument about the "Scandinavian character of Anglian England,"[39] and are diagnostic of Anglian identity in early England.[40] Some wrist clasps (Type A) were of wound wire, with linked spirals forming a hook that matched a loop formed similarly and attached to the opposite side of a sleeve slit. A metal plate version (Type B7), with latch and catch parts, became the most common in Anglian England.[41] Significantly, the area of use of these clasps ended abruptly on what was later defined as the political border between kingdoms of the Angles to the north and Saxons to the south.[42]

All of the English wrist clasp types share this distribution.[43] The women's jewelry seems to have marked not just an ethnic but also a political territory, increasing the likelihood that a new kind of disciplinary authority was operating. Another aspect of this development is quite striking. Wrist clasps came to have a higher "status index" than the brooches that had been serving as symbols of patrilineal families.[44] The higher status may indicate a social network with a new level of complexity emerging.

The wrist clasp fashion arrived in England by the last quarter of the fifth century, apparently as part of a migration of immigrants from southwest Norway to Humberside and/or Norfolk.[45] Although B-type clasps had been worn by men and women and used variously as garment fasteners, in a "more rule-bound" development in England, they appear to have become exclusively a female item employed principally as sleeve closures.[46] About 350 wrist clasps were known from all of Scandinavia as of

Figure 9.2 Specific kinds of sleeve fasteners characterized an "Anglian" female costume [drawn by Christine Wetherell].
Source: Gale R. Owen-Crocker, *Dress in Anglo-Saxon England,* Rev. Ed. (Woodbridge: Boydell, 2004), Fig. 32.

1984, while over 600 examples had been found in Anglian England.[47] The spread of wrist clasps was a "political development—a new movement looking for new forms of expression. ... The sixth century sees the consolidation of clasps as ... in effect, a national dress of Anglian England" for women.[48]

Scull thought that an intermittent wider regional power might have been exercised in East Anglia by groups or individuals who linked local internally ranked communities. Advised by the late J. M. Dodgson of "the high proportion of place-names in *–ingas* in Norfolk" he supposed a regional East Anglian authority might have grown on that base.[49] The surmise seems confirmed by Margaret Gelling's statement that by "the time of [early seventh-century king] Redwald the whole of his kingdom was partitioned among groups known [with names containing *–ingas* or *–inga-* suffixes] as 'followers of x' or 'dwellers at x'."[50] The incongruity of a patronymic ending ("sons of x," "male descendants of x") applied to a first lexical element that was not a personal name disappears if the suffix identified a community of families organized on a patrilineal principle.[51] Gelling's assessment would seem to indicate that communities on that model had become the administrative units of the Anglo-Saxon kingdom by Redwald's time.[52]

D-bracteates, *Beowulf*, and Patriliny

Five coastal *fylker*—roughly counties—of Norway have been pointed to as possible source for the forms of wrist clasps that came to represent Anglian England.[53] At their center are *fylker* Hordaland and Rogaland. This locale was one area where production and reception of Scandinavian gold D-bracteates were concentrated.[54] Scandinavian gold bracteates are pendants whose bestowal marked alliances at a high level of Germanic society. The more-than-a-thousand examples currently known were created from roughly the mid-fifth to mid-sixth century. Almost four hundred are of a particular kind. The embossed image of D-bracteates depicts the defeat of a monster.[55] If ever we would *expect* monster tales to have been current in Germanic Europe, it would be when D-bracteates were created and given. Thus we may look to this period for the origin of the monster stories of *Beowulf*. That all of the several dozen *Beowulf* analogues have connection with areas of D-bracteate concentration provides confirmation. I elaborated this analysis in a paper on the dating of *Beowulf*[56] and cite it here as warrant for looking to some lines of the *Beowulf* poem as a context for the wrist clasps being brought to England about the time D-bracteates were in circulation.

To see Grendel's arm hanging from Heorot hall, the Danish king's choice men are gathered, as well as the queen and a "troop of women" (*mægþa hose*, l. 924).[57] I believe it is the only time women appear in a group. Hrōðgār announces: "Indeed, [she] may say—/ whichever woman this son bore/ according to men-kin [i.e., into male kinship], if she yet lives—/ that to her the ancient-lord was kind/ about childbearing."[58]

The fourth edition of Klaeber's *Beowulf* describes this passage as "a felicity attributed to the hero's mother."[59] But in fact no praise is given to her at all. Instead, if she is alive, she has reason to be glad about the male kinship system. I believe the lines should be understood as probably the earliest instance of patriarchal tokenism in English literature. The fourth edition editors suggest that *æfter gumcynnum* is a cheville, a filler expression, with little meaning except as the empty phrase, "among humankind" "as *gum-* is not a rigorously gendered term."[60] However, the first words out of Beowulf's mouth include the lexeme, where we would hardly expect a cheville: "*Wē synt gumcynnes Ġēata lēode*" (l. 260). In 1991 I took this for a belligerent espousal of patriliny: "We are of male kin, people of the Geats!"[61] The declaration "We are of humankind, people of the Geats!" seems hardly possible. These passages support the inference that a disciplinary tendency about patrilineal kinship was brought to Anglian England along with D-bracteates and wrist clasps.[62]

Conclusions: Reading Signals

Mistakes can follow from "assuming that women were passive bearers of ethnic identity."[63] Women "could benefit from their association with [the] masculine power structure through displaying [its] gifted objects."[64] More complicated responses were also possible, vividly demonstrated in Suzanne Hakenbeck's reading of the signals involved in slight variations of female costume in Munich area cemeteries. Hakenbeck demonstrated that "local differences in the way brooches were pinned created a sense of opposition to funerary customs in other cemeteries and thereby a sense of local identity ... Subversive counter currents," she said, "were active."[65]

The adornment of a sleeved garment with metal cuff fasteners in England during the late fifth through mid-sixth centuries became an emblem of female prestige, of ethnic identity and a new political construct. Adopted after cultural competition over several generations among Germanic immigrants to that part of Britain, the practice identified an Anglian female. The jewelry came from Scandinavia, but new rules governed its use: only by women, and only on sleeves. The cultural inscription probably included a Scandinavian origin legend for the male spouse or parent and a claim by upper-level political leaders of descent from a war god. Proliferation of place names of patronymic type probably indicates the formal constitution of communities as groups of patrilineal families, a complete reversal of the principle of tribal composition seen in *matres* inscriptions. The monster-fighting motif of D-bracteates was represented in East Anglia not only in gold and other metals, but also, and very unusually, by a die and a possible patrix for manufacturing such pendants. Hero Beowulf's first words avow patriliny, as does Hrōðgār's speech on behalf of Beowulf's mother.

During the last phase at Spong Hill, as the wrist clasp fashion was accelerating, the cemetery saw the construction of barrows to mark the burial of eminent individuals. While wealthier, the grave goods in these barrows were not especially remarkable. However, the barrows raised there, a century before the monumental kingly ship burial at Sutton Hoo, are among the earliest English examples.[66] A patrilineal nation was being constructed.

Acknowledgments

I am grateful to Francis Battaglia and greenrocketdigital.com for production of the figures.

Frank Battaglia Emeritus Professor of English at the College of Staten Island, CUNY.

Notes

1. Tania M. Dickinson, "Translating Animal Art: Salin's Style I and Anglo-Saxon Cast Saucer Brooches," *Hikuin* 29 (2002): 180; Toby Martin, "Women, Knowledge and Power: The Iconography of Early Anglo-Saxon Cruciform Brooches," *Anglo-Saxon Studies in Archaeology and History* [hereafter *ASSAH*] 18 (2013): 2.
2. John Hines, "The Dating of Early Anglo-Saxon Graves and Grave Goods," in *Anglo-Saxon Graves and Grave Goods of the 6th and 7th Centuries AD: A Chronological Framework*, ed. John Hines and Alex Bayliss (London: Society for Medieval Archaeology Monograph 33, 2013), 517.
3. Sam Lucy, "Gender and Gender Roles," in *Oxford Handbook of Anglo-Saxon Archaeology*, ed. Helena Hamerow, David A. Hinton, and Sally Crawford (Oxford: Oxford University Press, 2011), 689. "Patrilocal exogamous intermarriage" is said, for example, to have brought to Kent the "possible Frankish marriage bride" with three radiate-headed brooches in grave 86 at Mill Hill, Deal: Stuart Brookes and Sue Harrington, *The Kingdom and People of Kent AD 400–1066* (Stroud, Gloucestershire: History Press, 2010), 49.
4. Lucy, "Gender Roles," 689.
5. Tania M. Dickinson, "Early Saxon Saucer Brooches: A Preliminary Overview," *ASSAH* 6 (1993): 39; John Hines states that "That female dress-accessories especially should take on [the] function [of asserting ethnic identity], in circumstances in which female exogamy is assumed to have been normal, is an issue that merits attention," in Hines, "Culture Groups and Ethnic Groups in Northern Germany In and Around the Migration Period," *Studien zur Sachsenforschung* [hereafter *SfurS*] 13 (1999): 227.
6. I argued for this "chronological depth of field" in discussion of similarities between Germanic and Celtic cultures observed by H. R. Ellis Davidson; see F. Battaglia, "Goddess Religion in the Early British Isles," in *Varia on the Indo-European Past*,

ed. Miriam Robbins Dexter and Edgar C. Polomé (Washington, DC: Journal of Indo-European Studies Monograph 19, 1997), 49–50.
7. H. M. Chadwick, *Origin of the English Nation* (Cambridge: Cambridge University Press 1907; reprinted 1956), 344. He astutely used matrilocal residence (which he termed "Beena marriage") as evidence of matriliny (330–333). See Kathleen Gough, "Variation in Matrilineal Systems," in *Matrilineal Kinship*, ed. David Schneider and K. Gough (Berkeley: University of California Press, 1974), 552–553. For other Germanic references, see Frank Battaglia, "The Germanic Earth Goddess in *Beowulf*?" *Mankind Quarterly* 31, no. 4 (1991): 417–426.
8. H. M. Chadwick, *Early Scotland* (Cambridge: Cambridge University Press, 1949), 117–118; Frank Battaglia, "A Common Background to Lai de Graelent and Noínden Ulad?" *Emania* 11 (1993): 41–48.
9. For Celts, Romans, Greeks see Chadwick, *Early Scotland*, 94–95; for Greeks: H. M. Chadwick, *Heroic Age* (Cambridge: Cambridge University Press, 1912), 357–361, further supported in Bella Zweig, "The Primal Mind: Using Native American Models for the Study of Women in Ancient Greece," in *Feminist Theory and the Classics*, ed. Nancy Sorkin Rabinowitz and Amy Richlin (New York: Routledge, 1993), 148. For early Europe, including Celts, see also Battaglia, "Goddess Religion," 49–50.
10. Chadwick, *Early Scotland*, 89–98.
11. "Epilogue," in *The Prehistory of Orkney*, ed. C. Renfrew (Edinburgh: Edinburgh University Press, 1985; reprinted 1990), 250–251.
12. Frank Battaglia, "The Matriliny of the Picts," *Mankind Quarterly* 31, nos. 1 & 2 (1990): 17–43.
13. Fredrik Hallgren, "Lineage Identity and Pottery Design," in *Form, Function and Context: Material Culture Studies in Scandinavian Archaeology*, ed. Deborah Olausson and Helle Vandkilde (Stockholm: Almqvist & Wiksell, 2000), 186.
14. Frank Battaglia, "A Neolithic Origin for the Collective Female Deities, the *Dísir*" (paper presented at the 47th International Congress on Medieval Studies, Western Michigan University, May 2012).
15. D. H. Green, *Language and History in the Early Germanic World* (Cambridge: Cambridge University Press, 1998), 34.
16. Brian Murdoch and Malcolm Kevin Read, *Early Germanic Literature and Culture* (Rochester, NY: Camden House, 2004), 87.
17. Philip A. Shaw, *Pagan Goddesses in the Early Germanic World, Eostre, Hreda and the Cult of the Mothers* (London: Bristol Classical, 2011), 45; Ton Derks, "The Perception of the Roman Pantheon by a Native Elite: The Example of Votive Inscriptions from Lower Germany," in *Images of the Past, Studies on Ancient Societies in Northwestern Europe*, ed. Nico Roymans and Franz Theuws (Amsterdam: Universiteit van Amsterdam, 1991), 235–265; P. Herz, "Einheimische Kulte und ethnische Strukturen. Methodische Überlegungen am Beispiel der Provinzen Germania inferior, Germania superior und Belgica," in *Labor omnibus unus*, ed. Heinz E. Herzig and Regula Frei-Stolba (Stuttgart: Steiner, 1989), 206–218.
18. Battaglia, "Matriliny of the Picts," 26–30.
19. "The 'hut-circles' within the Dartmeet system, and in other parallel systems, were not distributed evenly, but in clusters ... settlement clusters—or neighborhood groups, as I have come to call them"; Andrew Fleming, *The Dartmoor Reeves* (London: Batsford, 1988), 62. For British coaxial systems, see Tom Williamson, *Environment, Society and Landscape in Early Medieval England* (Rochester, NY: Boy-

dell, 2013), 94–106; for northwest Europe, see Leo Webley, *Iron Age Households, Structure and Practice in Western Denmark, 500 BC–AD 200* (Moesgaard: Jutland Archaeological Society, 2008), 42.

20. In large and small villas alike, Smith said, "kin-groups retained ... a fundamental bipartite structure, within each part of which a number of units of consumption or conjugal families existed" (New York: Routledge, 1997), 282. Tom Williamson agreed with Smith that Gayton Thorpe villa suggests "joint ownership of an estate by related families": *The Origins of Norfolk* (Manchester: Manchester University Press, 1993), 44.
21. Smith, *Roman Villas*, 240.
22. Spatial patterns of souterrains among the Picts north of the Firth of Tay during the Roman and sub-Roman periods suggest they had four such sub-groups; see Battaglia, "Matriliny of the Picts," 28.
23. Christopher Scull, "Burial Practice in Anglo-Saxon England," in Hines and Bayliss, *Chronological Framework*, 528.
24. Scull, "Burial Practice," 526.
25. Lotte Hedeager, "Migration Period Europe: The Formation of a Political Mentality," in *Rituals of Power*, ed. Frans Theuws and Janet L. Nelson (Boston: Brill, 2000), 15–57; Eric John, "The Point of Woden," *ASSAH* 5 (1992): 127–134. In England, "earl[y] Frankish material culture does not seem to have enjoyed the same cultural caché attached to Scandinavian-influenced material"; Sue Harrington and Martin Welch, *The Early Anglo-Saxon Kingdoms of Southern Britain AD 450–650* (Oxford: Oxbow, 2014), 182. On the reorganization of ethnicities, see Frank Battaglia, "*Sib* in *Beowulf*," *In Geardagum* 20 (1999): 27–47.
26. Nick Stoodley, "Burial Rites, Gender and the Creation of Kingdoms: The Evidence from Seventh-Century Wessex," *ASSAH* 10 (1999): 100.
27. Stoodley, "Burial rites," 101. "The major pattern ... in early Anglo-Saxon gendered grave furnishing" has been described as the "use of restricted sets of grave-goods, mainly limited to certain adult males and females, but with some adaptations for those aged 12 and over, and sometimes a concomitant decline in gender signaling in older age groups"; Lucy, "Gender Roles," 694. Comparably, saucer brooches were: "found with women, and in nearly every case these are late adolescents or adults, indicating a 'threshold of acquisition' exactly comparable with access to shields and/or swords among weapon-bearing men"; Dickinson, "Early Saxon," 38. Among the few exceptions to the sexually binary distribution of grave goods is female burial 1105 from Spong Hill, Norfolk, which contained a sword pommel; Catherine Hills, "Did the People of Spong Hill Come from Schleswig-Holstein?" *SfurS* 11 (1998): 152.
28. John Hines, "The Archaeological Study of Early Anglo-Saxon Cemeteries," 31, and "Implications for Anglo-Saxon Social History: Society and Gender," 528, in Hines and Bayliss, *Chronological Framework*.
29. Stoodley, "Burial Rites," 100; Dawn Hadley, "Negotiating Gender, Family and Status in Anglo-Saxon Burial Practices, c. 600–950," in *Gender in the Early Medieval World, East and West, 300–900*, ed. Leslie Brubaker and Julia M. H. Smith (Cambridge: Cambridge University Press, 2004), 302.
30. Catherine Hills and Sam Lucy, *Spong Hill Part IX: Chronology and Synthesis* (Cambridge: McDonald Institute, 2013), 259–264.
31. Frank Battaglia, "Cannibalism in *Beowulf* and Older Germanic Religion," in *The Anglo-Saxons: The World Through Their Eyes*, ed. Gale R. Owen-Crocker and

Brian W. Schneider (Oxford: Archaeopress, British Archaeological Reports, British Series 595, 2014), 141–148.
32. "Fabric 10," Hills and Lucy, *Spong Hill*, Appendix 5, 365–407; "bone ash," 160.
33. Mary Chester-Kadwell, *Early Anglo-Saxon Communities in the Landscape of Norfolk* (Oxford: Archaeopress, British Archaeological Reports, British Series 481, 2009), 161.
34. Hadley, "Negotiating Gender," 302.
35. Scull, "Burial Practice," 525.
36. We have indications that youth or advanced age caused a decline in the marking of gender. Additionally, "even under the wide umbrella of 'female gender identity,' a large amount of variation is seen, which presumably relates to other aspects of social identity: cultural associations may play a part in this, but so also do age, position on the social hierarchy, and perhaps marital status"; Lucy, "Gender Roles," 693.
37. Gale R. Owen-Crocker, "Dress and Identity," in Hamerow, Hinton, and Crawford, *Oxford Handbook*, 99–100, figure 7.1.b; Hines, "Culture Groups," 230.
38. "Annular brooches and small-long brooches, and square-headed and cruciform brooches were 'functional equivalents' of each other"; Lucy, "Gender Roles," 693. "A grammar of costume elements" provided a repertoire "from which particular artifacts [could] be chosen to signify a particular age-gender status"; Joanna Sofaer Derevenski, "Rings of Life: The Role of Early Metalwork in Mediating the Gendered Life Course," *World Archaeology* 31, no. 3 (2000): 394.
39. John Hines, *Scandinavian Character of Anglian England*, British Series 124 (Oxford: British Archaeological Reports, 1984).
40. Kenneth Penn and Birte Brugman, *Aspects of Anglo-Saxon Burial: Morning Thorpe, Spong Hill, Bergh Apton and Westgarth Gardens*, East Anglian Archaeology 119 (Dereham: Norfolk Museums and Archaeological Service), 7.
41. Hines, *Scandinavian Character*, figure 2.1.
42. Ibid., 275. On problems of identifying the territory of the East Anglian kingdom, see Tom Williamson, *Sutton Hoo and Its Landscape, The Context of Monuments* (Oxford: Oxbow, 2008), 123–126.
43. Tom Williamson, "East Anglia's Character and the 'North Sea World'," in *East Anglia and Its North Sea World in the Middle Ages*, ed. David Bates and Robert Liddiard (Woodbridge: Boydell, 2013), 55. Within Britain Anglian wrist clasps show minor dispersal outside this "homeland" area; Martin Carver et al., *Wasperton* (New York: Boydell, 2009), 79. This is much different from "Saxon" saucer brooches, which are broadly distributed outside the "the Saxon homeland of the Elbe-Weser triangle"; Hines, "Culture Groups," 227. For England, see Sam Lucy, *The Anglo-Saxon Way of Death* (Stroud: Sutton, 2000), 136, figure 5.6a. Karen Høilund Nielsen provided an overview of regional variation in early Anglo-Saxon costume in "The Schism of Anglo-Saxon Chronology," in *Burial & Society, The Chronological and Social Analysis of Archaeological Burial Data*, ed. Claus Kjeld Jensen and K. H. Nielsen (Aarhus: Aarhus University Press, 1997), 85, figure 23.
44. Penn and Brugman, *Aspects*, 90, table 7.2, 92.
45. "One dominant line of connection" between Norway and England along with another tentative strand of influence from Gotland was how the situation was summarized in John Hines, *Clasps, Hektespenner, Agraffen* (Stockholm: Almqvist and Wiksell, 1993), 88. For textile evidence of Migration Period connection see

Lisa Bender Jørgensen, *Northern European Textiles until AD 1000* (Aarhus: Aarhus University Press, 1992), 36, 95. Andreas Rau has expanded the corpus of type B 1 clasps from South Scandinavia in *Nydam Mose: Die personengebunden Gegenstände, Grabungen, 1989–1999*, Vols. 1 & 2 (Moesgård: Jysk Arkæologisk Selskab, 2010), 1: 125–145; 2: 51–59, and thus increased the likelihood of influence on Anglian England from that direction: Hills and Lucy, *Spong Hill*, 57; J. Hines, "The Origins of East Anglia in a North Sea Zone," in *East Anglia*, ed. Bates and Liddiard, 25–29.

46. Hines, *Scandinavian Character*, 108; Hines, *Clasps*, 82; Hills and Lucy, *Spong Hill*, 54.
47. Hines, *Scandinavian Character*, 307–334, Lists 2.1, 2.2, 72–73; a similar catalogue in Hines, *Clasps*, 109–126. Rau excavated about seventy-five "hook and eye fasteners" (similar to Type B wrist clasps that would be worn by Anglian women) in the clothing of male attackers whose defeat was celebrated in the Nydam bog deposits of weapons; he analyzed them along with about forty others discovered in Scandinavia in the last two decades: *Nydam Mose* 2: 5–6.
48. Hines, *Clasps*, 94, 92.
49. Christopher Scull, "Before Sutton Hoo: Structures of Power and Society in Early East Anglia," in *The Age of Sutton Hoo*, ed. Martin Carver (Rochester, NY: Boydell, 1992), 20. Joost Kuurman found a much higher frequency of *–ingahām* names in the East Midlands than in Kent: "An Examination of the *–ingas, –inga-* Place-Names in the East Midlands," *Journal of the English Place Name Society* 7 (1974): 15–16.
50. Margaret Gelling, "A Chronology for Suffolk Place-Names," in Carver, *Age of Sutton Hoo*, 55.
51. Richard Coates, "The Plural of Singular *-ing*: an Alternative Application of Old English *–ingas*," in *Names, Places and People, An Onomastic Miscellany in Memory of John McNeal Dodgson*, ed. Alexander R. Rumble and A. D. Mills (Stamford: Watkins, 1997), 28.
52. Barrie Cox proposed a sixth-century date for the beginning of *–ingas* place-names: "*–Ingas, –Inga Names*," in *Wiley Blackwell Encyclopedia of Anglo-Saxon England*, 2nd ed., ed. Michael Lapidge, John Blair, Simon Keynes, Donald Scragg (New York: Wiley-Blackwell, 2013), 257. In general, *–ingahām* names were earlier; Kuurman, "Examination."
53. Hines, *Scandinavian Character*, 105, 282; *Clasps*, 88; see also note 45.
54. Find-spots of D-bracteates known as of 2005: Axboe, *Brakteatstudier* (København: Kongelige Nordiske Oldskriftselskab, 2007), figure 52.
55. Alexandra Pesch distinguished types of D-bracteates and provided maps of their distributions: *Die Goldbrakteaten der Völkerwanderungszeit—Thema und Variation* (Berlin: De Gruyter, 2007), 240–319.
56. Frank Battaglia, "*Beowulf* and the Bracteates" (presented at the Harvard University conference "The Dating of *Beowulf*: A Reassessment," September 2011).
57. R. D. Fulk, Robert E. Bjork, and John D. Niles, *Klaeber's Beowulf*, 4th ed. (Toronto: University of Toronto Press, 2008). All references to this edition.
58. *Hwæt, þæt secgan mæġ/ efne swā hwylċ mæġþa swā ðone magan cende/ æfter gumcynnum, ġyf hēo ġȳt lyfað,/ þæt hyre ealdmetod ēste ware/ bearnġebyrdo* (ll. 942b – 946a).
59. Ibid., 173.
60. Ibid., 345, 388, 173.
61. Battaglia, "Earth Goddess," 426.

62. D-type bracteates in various metals, a possible D-bracteate die and D-bracteate patrix, as well as other monster-fighting bracteates have been found in East Anglia: Charlotte Behr and Tim Pestell, "The Bracteate Hoard from Binham—An Early Anglo-Saxon Central Place?" *Medieval Archaeology* 58 (2014): 44–77. The gold D-bracteate (IK 601), with a design like the possible patrix, has its closest parallel in North Jutland, Denmark, although a related example (IK 605) was found in Rogaland, Norway—Pesch, *Die Goldbrakteaten*, 286–922. The B-type monster-fighting bracteates (IK 604,1,2) closely resemble seven die-identical bracteates probably from Schleswig-Holstein, Germany: Behr and Pestell, "Bracteate Hoard," 54.
63. Bonnie Effros, "Dressing Conservatively: Women's Brooches as Markers of Ethnic Identity?" in Brubaker and Smith, *Gender in Early Medieval World*, 165–184.
64. Martin, "Women, Knowledge," 11.
65. Susanne E. Hakenbeck, "Situational Ethnicity and Nested Identities: New Approaches to an Old Problem," *ASSAH*, 14 (2007): 25–26.
66. Hills and Lucy, *Spong Hill*, 271.

Index

Adaptation, 76, 80, 87
Adelaide of Turin, 4, 9
Adultery, 25, 33, 52, 61, 65
Aetius, 49, 51
Afterlife, 49, 53, 55–56, 59
Age, 61–62, 64, 69, 72, 87, 89, 91, 94–95, 115, 119, 124–127
Agency, x, 34, 76, 78, 80, 83–84
Alexander III, Pope, 26–27
Alfonso X, king of Castile, 38, 46–47
Alfred, king of Wessex, 96, 100
Amis & Amiloun, 53, 59, 113
Animals, 75–76, 78–81, 83–84, 86, 96, 98, 115
Aquinas, Thomas, 37, 39, 42, 45
Archery, 91, 94, 98
Aretaios, 51–52
Arthur, King, 76–77, 82, 87, 104–113

Battles
    Bremule (1119), 96
    Lincoln (1217), 96
    Northampton (1264), 92
Beata de Piedrahita, 43
Beatrice of Tuscany, 11
Becket, Saint Thomas, 55
Beowulf
    Grendel, 118, 121
    Heorot, 121
    Hroðgar, 121–122
Berenguela de Anglesola y Pinós, 38
Bernard of Clairvaux, 57

Bevis of Hampton, 106–107, 113
Bible
    Old Testament, 14, 17, 54, 65, 68
Blanca de Aragón y de Anjou (Blanche of Anjou, queen of Aragon), 40, 46
Breton Lays, 5, 75, 87, 113
Brooch, 120
Burial
    Cremation, 119
    Funerary rites, 117–118
    Furnished, 114, 117–118
    Horse, vii, 77–78, 81–83, 86, 92, 98, 117–118

Caffarini, Tommaso, 39, 46
Cannibalism, 118, 125
Canon law, 22, 37
Catherine of Siena, 39, 43
Ceramic, vii, 115, 118–119
Charlemagne, 12
Charles V, king of France, 91
Charles, count of Flanders, 93, 99
Chastity, 15–17
Chaucer
    Canterbury Tales, vii, 5, 50, 53, 57, 59, 62–63, 67–71, 73
    Clerk's Tale, 62, 67–71, 73–74
    Franklin's Tale, 68, 74
    Knight's Tale, 68
    Merchant's Tale, v, vii, 61–63, 67–74
    Shipman's Tale, 62, 68–69, 73–74
    Summoner's Tale, 57, 72

Troilus and Criseyde, 102, 109, 111, 113
Wife of Bath's Tale, 62, 67
Chivalry, vi, 88, 97–99
Chrétien de Troyes, 95
Constance of France, 25–26
Corpus Christi, v, vii, 35–45, 47
Council of Lyon (583), 54
Council of Trent, 42–43
Courtly Romance, 61
Cunibert, bishop of Turin, 11, 13, 20

D Bracteate, 121, 128
Damian, Peter, 4, 8–9, 17–18
Dante, Divine Comedy, 54
de Ayala, Inés, 43
de Vitry, Jacques, 55
Death, xi, 4, 10, 23–25, 27–30, 49, 51–53, 55–56, 59, 89, 94, 96, 98, 102, 106, 108–111, 113, 118, 126
Deborah, 14, 124
Decay, 49–50, 53, 56
Denasti, 51–52
Denmark
Funen Island, 118
Disease, 48–51, 53, 56–58, 60
dísir, 116, 118, 124
Divine, 11, 32, 37, 56, 64, 98
Dress, 82, 115, 117, 120–121, 123, 126

East Anglia (Anglian), 32, 34, 72, 115, 117, 119–122, 126–128
Edward III, king of England, 91
England
Buckinghamshire, High Wycombe, St Margaret's, 49, 57
Chichester, Hospital of St James & St Mary, 49, 57
Faversham, 24
Gloucestershire, Marshfield, 116
Higham, Lillechurch Priory, vii, 24, 29–30, 32, 34
Humberside, 120
Norfolk, Spong Hill, 117–121, 125–126
Romsey Abbey, 21, 24, 32–33
St Albans, St Julian's Hospital, 53, 59
Stratford-at-Bow, St Leonard's Priory, 23
Suffolk, Sutton Hoo, 123, 126–127
Winchester, xi, 1, 6–7, 24, 31, 33, 49, 57, 90

Fainting, vi, 5, 101–102, 106–111
Fairy, 5, 75–87, 108, 113
Fashion, 120, 123
Feudalism, 50
Florence, count of Holland, 94
Fourth Lateran Council (1215), 55
France
Chalons, 94
Marseilles, St Cyr Monastery, 52
Montreuil, Sainte-Austreberthe, 27–28
Orbey, Unterlinden, 43, 47
Saint Sulpice-la-Forêt, 23
Savoy, 9, 13
Francis of Assisi, Saint, 37
Funnel Beaker Culture, 115

Gawain, 105, 107–110
Germany
Nuremberg, St Katherine, 39
Godfrey, margrave of Tuscany, 8
Guilbert de Tournai, 55
Guinevere, 75–79, 81–82, 85–87, 102, 108, 111

Henry II, king of England, 21–22, 24–25, 27–28, 32, 99
Henry III, Holy Roman Emperor, 9
Henry of Blois, bishop of Winchester, 24
Henry VIII, king of England, 91, 96
Hildegard von Bingen, 40
Homosociality, vi, 101, 103–104, 112
Horsemanship, 95
Hugh of Lincoln, Saint, 55, 59
Hugh of Saint-Cher, 37
Hugh of Tuscany, 9
Humbert of Romans, 42, 47, 55, 60
Hunting, 76, 78, 88, 90, 92, 95–96, 99–100

Innocent II, Pope, 93–94
Interdisciplinarity, 3
Italy
Ancona, 10, 12, 16, 19
Camerino, 12–13
Lodi, 10
Milan, San Eustorgio, 37
Naples, Santa Chiara, 38, 45
Pisa, San Domenico, 39–40, 46
Sierra Sant'Abbondio, Fonte Avellana, 9–10

Spoleto, 12–13
Turin, 4, 8–9, 11, 13, 18, 20
Tuscany, 4, 8–9, 11–13
Venice, 7, 41, 51

James I, king of Scotland, 91
James II, king of Scotland, 92
John XXII, Pope, 35, 94
Judith, 14–16, 34, 102, 106, 111
Juliana of Liége, 37
Kempe, Margery, 52, 59
King David (biblical), 10

Lancelot, 105, 108–110
Lanfrank of Bec, 50
Language, 5, 33, 61, 63–64, 66, 69, 71, 73, 76, 78–80, 85, 102, 104, 112, 124
Law, 6, 9–10, 12, 22, 25, 28, 32, 37, 85, 91, 104
Lechery, 52, 55–56
Leonor of Guzmán, 41
Leprosaria, 50, 53–56, 59
Leprosy, 48–60
Liminality, 49, 53
Living dead, 53–54
Louis VII, king of France, 27, 34

Male Gaze, vi, 5, 75–79, 81, 83–85, 87
Malory, Thomas, 105, 112–113
Mandeville, Geoffrey de, earl of Essex, 94
Marie, Countess of Boulogne, 21–34
Marriage, v, 4, 6, 9, 13, 22, 24–27, 30–31, 33, 61–65, 67–72, 111, 123–124
Marshal, William, 92, 99
Matilda of Boulogne, queen of England, 7, 21–26, 31
Matriliny, 115–116, 124–125
Matthew of Flanders, count of Boulogne, 21–22, 25–32
Merlin, 104
Mirk, John, 50
Moore, Robert, 52
Moral, v, 9, 12–13, 49, 51, 53, 56, 61, 63, 65, 68, 72
Munio de Zamora, 38

Neolithic, 115, 124
Nicholas II, Pope, 10, 12

Norway
Hordaland, 121
Rogaland, 121, 128
Nose, 49, 51–52, 56, 58–59

Otto III, Holy Roman Emperor, 12, 14

Patriliny, vi, 5, 114–115, 117, 119, 121–123, 125, 127
Pedro I, king of Castile, 36, 40
Pérez de Ayala, Fernán, 41
Performativity, 110
Philip III, king of France, 94
Picts, 115, 124–125
Place-names, 115, 121, 127
Play, 33, 80, 88–92, 97–98, 101, 126
Pluto, 67, 73
Politics, 6, 27, 34, 60, 78, 112–113
Proserpina, 67
Purgatory, 53, 55–57, 59

Queenship, x, xii

Raimondo de Capua, 39
Raptus, 4, 22, 25, 30–31, 33
Rawcliffe, Carole, 59–60
Raymond of Peñafort, 39
Raymond V, count of Toulouse, 25
Redwald, king of East Anglia, 121
Richard I, king of England, 99
Richard II, king of England, 92
Robert of Clermont, 94
Rolle, Richard, 52, 59
Round Table, 104–105, 109–110

Saint Louis of France (Louis IX, king of France), 55, 60
Sancia of Majorca, 38
Savonarola, 43
Schwesterbuch, 39
Scotland
Coldingham Priory, 52
Second Council of Lyon (1274), 53
Semantics, 63–64, 68–69
Settlements, 29, 116, 119, 124
Sex/Sexuality
Homosexuality, 75, 86
Shakespeare, William
Troilus and Cressida, 51, 52
Sins, 28, 54–56
Social death, 49

Sontag, Susan, 52, 59
Souls, 30
Spain
    Ávila, Santa Catalina, 43
    Barcelona, 35, 39, 46
    Benavente, Sancti Spiritus, 43
    Bilbao, Nuestra Señora de la Encarnación, 43
    Cáceres, San Miguel de Trujillo, 43, 46
    Caleruega, Santo Domingo, 38, 41–42, 45–46
    Lekeitio, Santo Domingo, 43
    Madrid, Santo Domingo el Real, 38, 40, 43
    Medina del Campo, Santa María la Real, 43, 47
    Quejana, San Juan Baptista, Chapel of the Virgen del Cabello, vii, 41–42, 46
    Salamanca, Nuestra Señora de la Consolación, 42–43, 45–47
    Segovia, Santo Domingo, 42
    Sigena, Santa María, 40
    Tamarite de Litera, 39, 46
    Toledo, Madre de Dios, 44
    Toledo, Santo Domingo, vii, 35–36, 41–47
    Toro, 42
    Vallbona de les Monges, 36, 38–39, 44
    Zamora, Santa María de las Dueñas, 38, 45

Stagel, Elsbeth, 39
Statutes
    Cambridge (1388), 91
    Winchester (1285), 90
Stephen, king of England, 21–23, 25–26, 29, 31
Supernatural, 77–78, 80, 84
Sweden
    Alvastra, Alvastra Pile Dwelling, 116
    Skogmossen, Västmanland, 115
Swords, 95, 125

Theobald, archbishop of Canterbury, 23–24, 32
Theodosius, emperor of Rome, 12, 14
Theology, 49, 53, 56
Thing, 53, 92, 97, 116
Third Lateran Council (1179), 54
Tournaments, 5, 92–95, 99
Treasury of Merit, 54
Tristan and Isolde, 51–52

Villa, viii, 46–47, 116, 125
Violence, 6, 10, 12, 17, 19, 32, 89–91, 97–98, 105

Walker Bynum, Caroline, 55, 60
War, 23, 88–89, 91–97, 105, 122
Wichman, archbishop of Madgeburg, 94
Wrist clasps, vi, 5, 114–115, 117, 120–123, 125–127

www.ingramcontent.com/pod-product-compliance
Lightning Source LLC
Chambersburg PA
CBHW070045120526
44589CB00035B/2319